Contents

Foreword

In 1994, I advised (with Helen Mountfield) the Association of Teachers and Lecturers on the legal implications of the Department for Education Circular on 'Sex Education in Schools'. Recent correspondence in a national Sunday newspaper disclosed that ours had not been the only opinion solicited on this subject: Now the National Children's Bureau has published a comprehensive survey on the subject, which validates the Old Latin tag 'Tot homines, quot sententiae' – in 1996 more acceptably translated as 'There are as many opinions as there are persons'.

What may at first blush be seen as a marginal, even an exotic subject, to excite academic interest, in fact raises issues of considerable legal complexity and social importance. Although, prior to the Education (No.2) Act 1986, there were no specific obligations resting with schools or local education authorities concerning either the provision of sex education or its content, in the wake of the Education Act 1993, the provision of sex education is compulsory for children of secondary school age, subject only to parental right of exemption.

And therein lies the rub. To state that children's rights end where parents' rights begin may be to exaggerate: but there is certainly no necessary coincidence of the interests of each. In the historic *Gillick* case, Lord Scarman said that at common law 'parental rights are defined from parental duty and exist only so long as they are needed for the protection of the person and property of the children'; but the tendency of modern education legislation has been to treat parents as consumers with the right to choose – in contradiction, for example, to the policy which underlies the Children Act 1989, which treats children as persons with autonomous rights. Moreover a parent's ability to deny a child access to sex education may well breach the child's right to receive information and education under Article 10 of the European Convention on Human Rights and Article 2 of the First Protocol.

In *Gillick*, Lord Templeman said memorably: 'There are many things which a girl under 16 needs to practise, but sex is not one of them'. As to whether and how she (or her brother) should be taught about it, this book will provide the fullest possible answer.

Michael Beloff Q.C.

The contributors

Andrew Bainham is a lecturer in Law at the University of Cambridge, where he is a Fellow of Christ's College. A leading expert on the law relating to children, with numerous scholarly publications to his name, his books include *Children, Parents and the State* (Sweet and Maxwell, 1988) and (with Stephen Cretney) *Children: The Modern Law* (Family Law, 1993).

Lois Bibbings is a lecturer in Law at the University of Bristol with a special interest in socio-legal areas of research, including law and sexuality. Her publications include a chapter in *The Frontiers of Criminality* (ed. I. Loveland, Sweet and Maxwell, 1995).

Anthony Bradney is Senior Lecturer in Law and Sub-Dean of the Faculty of Law at the University of Leicester. He is an executive member of the Socio-Legal Studies Association and is a former Vice-President of the Association of Legal and Social Philosophy. He has a special interest in the relationship between religions and laws in Great Britain and has published widely on the subject, including *Religions, Rights and Laws* (Leicester University Press, 1993).

Jo Bridgeman is a lecturer in Law at the University of Liverpool and Convenor of the Faculty of Law's Feminist Legal Research Unit. She is a co-editor of *Law and Body Politics* (Dartmouth, 1995). She has a special research interest in the area of law and women's health and is currently working on projects on contraception and anorexia.

Neville Harris is Reader in Law and Associate Dean (Research) in the Faculty of Law at the University of Liverpool. His research interests lie in the field of Welfare Law. He is joint general editor of the *Journal of Social Security Law*, senior editor of the *Educa-*

Children, Sex Education and the Law

Examining the issues

The National Children's Bureau was established as a registered charity in 1963. Our purpose is to identify and to promote the interests of all children and young people and to improve their status in a diverse society.

We work closely with professionals and policy makers to improve the lives of all children but especially young children, those affected by family instability, children with special needs or disabilities and those suffering the affects of poverty and deprivation.

We collect and disseminate information about children and promote good practice in children's services through research, policy and practice development, publications, seminars, training and an extensive library and information service.

The Bureau works in partnership with Children in Scotland and Children in Wales.

ISBN 1 874579 66 0

Published by National Children's Bureau Enterprises Ltd, 8 Wakley Street, London EC1V 7QE. Telephone 0171 843 6000.

National Children's Bureau Enterprises is the trading company for the National Children's Bureau (registered charity number 258825).

Typeset by Books Unlimited (Nottm), NG19 7QZ

Printed and bound in the United Kingdom by Biddles Ltd

tion Law Reports and a member of the editorial board of *Education and the Law*. His publications include *Social Security for Young People* (Avebury, 1989), *Law and Education: Regulation, Consumerism and the Education System* (Sweet and Maxwell, 1993) and *The Law Relating to Schools* (2nd ed.) (Tolley, 1995).

Rachel Thomson is Senior Development Officer for the Sex Education Forum, based at the National Children's Bureau. The Forum, founded in 1987, is an umbrella body bringing together over 30 national organisations involved in school sex education. Rachel Thomson is also involved in research with young people and has published widely in this area with the Women, Risk and AIDS Project team. Her publications include *Learning About Sex* (Tufnell Press, 1991), *An Enquiry into Sex Education* (National Children's Bureau, 1992), *Religion, Ethnicity and Sex Education* (National Children's Bureau, 1993) and *Developing and Reviewing a School Sex Education Policy* (National Children's Bureau, 1994).

1. The regulation and control of sex education

Neville Harris, Reader in Law, the University of Liverpool

Introduction

Prior to the Education (No.2) Act 1986, there were no specific obligations resting with schools and local education authorities (LEAs) concerning the provision of sex education or its content. Under that Act, however, it became mandatory for school governing bodies both to determine their policy on whether sex education should form part of the secular curriculum and to ensure that, when sex education was given, moral values were promoted. Today, following the enactment of the Education Act 1993, sex education provision is compulsory for children of secondary school age, subject to a parental right of exemption in respect of their child. The changes made to the legal regime by the 1993 Act, and the issuing of subsequent guidance by the Department for Education[1] in 1994, have given this area increased importance, not only for children and young people themselves, but also for those who have responsibility for their education and decisions concerning it – especially teachers and parents, as well as those professionals who provide family support and health care.

In fact, this is now a complex area of law of practice, and the reforms present a wide range of legal questions, some of which are quite difficult. The overall aim of this chapter is to explain the development of the present legislation and official guidance on sex education in schools and to consider some of its key implications. My aim, and those of the authors of the chapters that follow, is also to inform discussion of the legal and wider issues arising from the regulation and control of sex education in schools and to guide professional practice.

The importance of the legal regime stems from the central role played by schools in the provision of sex education. There has, in recent years, been continuing concern about the quality of sex education provided by schools (see Thomson and Scott 1992; Oakley et al 1995). This was, until recently, reinforced by the omission of specific references to sex education in the *Framework for the Inspection of Schools* issued by OFSTED to inspectors carrying out school inspections under section 9 of the Education (Schools) Act 1992; a revised version of the *Framework*, published in October 1995, has remedied this (see *Times Educational Supplement*, August 11, 1995, p.4). However, the fact remains that schools are the principal source of information about sexual matters for adolescents. Knowledge of sexual matters gained through socialisation processes involving the transmission of knowledge from peers was regarded by just 29 per cent of 14–16-year-olds in one survey as the major source of information about sex, as compared with 63 per cent of the sample who regarded school teaching as the major source of information (Allen 1987, p.143). Wellings and others, whilst reporting a lower proportion of children who regarded sex education at school as the principal source of information, nevertheless conclude that 'the school has been playing an increasingly important role in the sexual education of the young' (Wellings and others 1995, p.418). This research has also confirmed the importance of sex education in influencing sexual behaviour among adolescents. The survey provides evidence that the age at which sexual intercourse begins is later among those males whose primary source of information about sex is sex education at school and that, for both sexes, sex education at school results in a greater likelihood of the use of contraception, notably a condom, when intercourse first occurs.

The central role played by schools has now been reinforced by a legal requirement (in the case of secondary school pupils and those at special schools who are of secondary school age) to provide sex education, which is now statutorily defined in addition to being surrounded by a pre-existing duty to ensure that it is provided with 'due regard to moral considerations and the value of family life' (s.46 of the Education (No.2) Act 1986). A new facet of consumer choice in the education system is the recently conferred right of parents to withdraw their children from sex education at school, other than where it is provided as part of the National Curriculum (see below). Under earlier legislation, which is still in force, there were merely opportunities for parents (but not, specifically, children) to complain about the way in which schools complied with their responsibilities and exercised their powers concerning sex education (see Harris 1993, pp.245–251).

The increasing regulation of this part of the school curriculum, as well as of the school curriculum in general, raises important issues of principle with regard to the power of the state to dictate and control the content of school education (see generally Coulby 1990, Meredith 1992, Graham and Tytler 1993 and Harris 1993). It is certainly necessary to view the evolution of the law on sex education, and to consider the implications, with a clear perception of the broad political context. Government policy has, amongst other things, aimed to bring the direction of the education system more firmly under central control, as exemplified by such developments as the introduction of the National Curriculum and the Funding Agency for Schools. The law on sex education confirms this trend, but it also reflects government interest in monitoring and publicising the extent of sexual activity among young people, and any resultant pregnancies and parenthood.

Indeed, part of the policy context is the way that the sexual behaviour of young people has, over recent years, been brought within the scope of the Government's broad national health strategy. The health Green Paper, *The Health of the Nation* (Secretary of State for Health 1991, Annex H para.H.19), set a target for 'improved sexual health, e.g. a reduction in pregnancies below the age of 16'. The subsequent White Paper (in July 1992) included a target reduction figure of 50 per cent in such under-age pregnancies by the year 2000 (from 9.5 per 1,000 girls aged 13-15 in 1989 to no more than 4.8) (Secretary of State for Health 1992, p.95). In April 1994 a health minister, Lady Cumberlege, reportedly backed health workers who used their discretion and professional judgement over the issuing of condoms to under-age children, which had provoked a political row (see 'Minister backs condoms for the under-16s', *The Guardian*, April 29, 1994). Young people's sexual behaviour has also been considered in the context of the lowering of the age of consent for male homosexual acts in private to 18 years, under the Criminal Justice and Public Order Act 1994 (s.143).

Sexual activity and parenthood among young people and young adults has also featured in many of the political debates about the responsibilities of absent fathers for maintenance of their offspring, for example in the context of the child support legislation (see Garnham and Knights 1993). Indeed it has been integral to many of the policy debates on public welfare support in recent years, such as those concerned with Government proposals to prevent homeless young people from having priority access to local authority housing (see Department of the Environment 1994), and, more especially, ministers' assertions that the benefits system might be encouraging teenage pregnancy (see 'Portillo fuels debate on benefits for single parents' *The Times*, 16 September, 1993). According to one press report,

> Ministers...are considering capping welfare and housing benefits to single mothers, whom they portrayed as feckless young parasites who get pregnant deliberately to jump housing queues and whose aim thereafter is to breed with abandon ... on income support ('Return of the Bogeywoman', *Independent on Sunday*, 10 October, 1993).

However, one recent social study of teenage pregnancy has produced results which 'do not support the notion that the young women intended to gain access to council housing by becoming pregnant and having a child' (Francombe and Walsh 1995, p. 19).

Given the moralistic thrust to many elements of government social policy relating to young parenthood and sexuality, which may be perceived as reflecting the Government's 'social and moral authoritarianism' (Whitty and Menter 1989, p. 253), it is unsurprising that sex education have received attention, in the form of legislation and official guidance to schools. Indeed, it has been suggested that parts of the Government's guidance have been 'no doubt ... influenced by its own view of the morality of sexual activity among the young' (Bainham 1993, p. 569; see below). Surprisingly, the need for a response by the Government to the increasing national concern about the spread of HIV/AIDS began to have a bearing on the development of the legislation on sex education only quite recently (although it was mentioned in the 1987 circular, referred to below); previously, most emphasis was placed on wide-ranging publicity campaigns, mostly targeted on the young, and on the development of proposals for a strategic health policy for the nation.

The development of the law and policy guidance on sex education prior to the Education Act 1993

The Education Acts 1944 and 1980

Until the Education Act 1993 there was no statutory duty on schools to provide sex education. The Education Act 1944 (s.23) gave control of the secular curriculum at schools to LEAs, who had a general duty (which still exists) (ss.7 and 8) to 'contribute towards the spiritual, moral, mental and physical development of the community' by securing 'efficient education' and had to ensure the provision of 'sufficient' schools for this purpose. This certainly *empowered* the provision of sex education by schools, who were generally left free to decide when, and in what context, sex education should be provided.

By the 1970s, many LEAs had clear sex education policies, at a time of growing sexual freedom among young people. Nevertheless, in some cases the inclusion of sex education was left to individual schools. Often the way that sex education was covered in the curriculum was, in any event, still determined at school level. After the Education Act 1980 had begun to usher in the present era of consumerism in education, with its provisions on parental school preference (see ss6-8), schools became subject to strict requirements on the publication of information, designed primarily to help parents in the selection of schools. Regulations imposing a duty on schools to publish information on provision included a requirement to provide information about the manner and context in which sex education was provided at the school (Education (School Information) Regulations 1981 (SI 1981 No.630), Sched.2). The Education (School Information) (England) Regulations 1994 (SI 1994 No.1421, as amended) now require instead a summary of the content and organisation of sex education to be included in the published information; and there is corresponding provision for Wales: SI 1994 No.2330.

The development of parental choice in relation to school admissions did not extend as far as the content of their child's education once the child was registered at a particular school. Of course, parents had a right under the 1944 Act to withdraw their children from religious education and collective worship and, if they could provide a suitable education, to educate their children 'otherwise' than at school (see s.36). These rights have continued, although the right of withdrawal from religious education and collective worship is now contained in the Education Reform Act 1988 (s.9(3)) and, in the case of special schools, the Education Act 1993 (s.188(6)). But there was no specific right of veto in respect of their child's sex education. Nevertheless, there was a general (although qualified) duty owed by local education authorities, under section 76 of the 1944 Act (still in force), to ensure that 'children are educated in accordance with the wishes of their parents'. The scope of section 76 has been tested in the courts, but not in relation to parental choice concerning the curriculum. In the section 76 cases, the courts have held that parental wishes do not have primacy and are merely among a range of factors to be considered by local education authorities when exercising their functions.[3] More recently the DFEE has argued that section 76 cannot override the provision of the statutory curriculum to a particular pupil (see below).

The Education (No.2) Act 1986

The pattern of legal control (such as it was) over the secular curriculum was left undisturbed until the Education (No.2) Act 1986. This removed LEA control by repealing section 23 of the 1944 Act (above). The 1986 Act gave effect to reforms outlined in the 1985 White Paper *Better Schools* (DES 1985), presented by the then Secretary of State for Education and Science, Sir Keith Joseph. This confirmed the Government's centralising tendencies. Indeed, the Department of Education and Science (the DES, whose education responsibility now rests with the Department for Education and Employment (DFEE), with the Welsh Office having responsibility for most national education matters in Wales) had been seeking to exert an ever-increasing influence over the school curriculum since the late 1970s (see Harris 1993, p. 199). The abolition in 1985 of the Schools Council, which represented teachers and LEAs, was seen as an important step towards centralisation of control over the school curriculum (see Plaskow 1988). Tighter legal control over the school curriculum, and increased central powers, had in fact been recommended by the House of Commons Education Select Committee in 1981 but had been rejected by the Government in 1982 (see Harris 1993, p. 199). However, *Better Schools* suggested that there had been a fundamental policy shift, even though its tone was largely pragmatic. Impetus for this change had undoubtedly resulted from ministers' increasing disquiet about perceived ideological excesses of particular LEAs, and especially the Inner London Education Authority (including its approach to homosexuality – see Macnair 1989, p. 36). The White Paper singled out Peace Studies for particular criticism (leading to sections 44 and 45 of the 1986 Act, which, in broad terms, sought to outlaw political bias in both teaching and extra-curricular activities organised by teachers).

Sex education was one of the areas singled out in *Better Schools*. Here the Government's concern centred on what it perceived to be an inadequate emphasis by teachers on the moral dimension to sexual matters covered by sex education. The Government stated (para.71) that 'health and sex education, taught within a moral framework, are a necessary preparation for responsible adulthood'. This approach was carried through into the 1986 Act, which provided (and still provides) that LEAs and governing bodies must

> take such steps as are reasonably practicable to secure that where sex education is given to any registered pupils at a school it is given in such

a manner as to encourage those pupils to have due regard to moral considerations and the value of family life (s. 46).

The moral tone was also reflected in the official guidance issued to schools and LEAs in 1987 (when the section came into operation) (DES Circular 11/87, *Sex Education at School*). It recommended that pupils should be 'encouraged to consider the importance of self-restraint, dignity and respect for themselves and others, and helped to recognise the physical, emotional and moral risks of casual and promiscuous sexual behaviour' (para.19). This clearly value-laden advice encouraged teachers to stress the benefits of stable married and family life (whilst also advising care not to cause upset to those from one parent families). Teachers were also told that they should not to advocate homosexual behaviour, present it as the 'norm' or encourage homosexual experimentation by pupils. This guidance predated the Local Government Act 1988, section 28 of which amended the Local Government Act 1986 to, *inter alia*, make it unlawful for *local authorities* to promote homosexuality or promote teaching of the acceptability of homosexuality as a 'pretended family relationship' in maintained schools.

It was also necessary for the official guidance to address the impact of *Gillick* v *West Norfolk and Wisbech AHA* [1985] 3 All ER 402 on the giving of contraceptive advice by teachers. Unfortunately, the guidance lacked precision, suggesting merely that the House of Lords' sanctioning of the giving of contraceptive advice to the under-16s by doctors in certain circumstances had 'no parallel' in the school context. This might or might not have been true, but even if it was correct the circular's implication that there the matter ended, reinforced by the advice that teachers should not allow concern for individual pupils who sought their advice on contraception to 'trespass on the proper exercise of parental rights and responsibilities', was erroneous. Further guidance has now been issued and is discussed by Bridgeman in Chapter 3. The implications of *Gillick* on the giving of advice by teachers is also considered in Chapter 3 and in Chapter 2, by Bainham.

Despite the increasing intervention by the Government in the area of sex education, schools and LEAs were still free to determine their own sex education policies. However, Government concern to promote better standards of education led to the inclusion in the 1986 Act of specified lines of responsibility for the secular curriculum, including sex education. LEAs were required to determine, keep under review, and maintain and circulate to schools, a statement of their policy on the secular curriculum (s.17). In voluntary aided schools (most of which are Roman Catholic), the governing body had to have regard to this statement but was otherwise free to determine its own policy on the secular curriculum (s.19). In other LEA-maintained schools, governing bodies had to consider the LEA's policy on the secular curriculum, and determine their own aims for the secular curriculum at their school and whether sex education should form part of it. In these schools the head teacher in turn had a duty to ensure that sex education provided at the school was compatible with the governors' policy, unless that policy was incompatible with a public examination syllabus (s.18) (see Chapter 5 by Bradney). All in all, therefore, there was shift in control from the LEA to the school (especially with the concomitant repeal of section 23 of the 1944 Act, noted above). Although there was no requirement to provide sex education, the 1987 Circular (at para.7) stressed the importance of schools offering 'some education about sexual matters'.

Education Reform Act 1988

The Education Reform Act 1988 transformed the secular curriculum, but until it was amended by the Education Act 1993 it was not concerned directly with sex education. It introduced the National Curriculum as part of a new 'basic curriculum' which most state-maintained schools in England and Wales would be required to follow. Schools had to provide both a 'balanced and broadly based' curriculum and one which included religious education. The significance of Part I, which contained the relevant provisions, is that it centralised (in the hands of the Secretary of State) control and direction of the school curriculum and gave rise to unprecedented regulation of the content of education.

The 1988 Act did not explicitly make the provision of sex education compulsory. However, it was argued (see Harris *et al.* 1992, p. 128) that the provision of sex education was clearly necessary if schools were to comply with their general duty to provide a basic curriculum which prepared pupils 'for the opportunities, responsibilities and experiences of adult life' (1988 Act, s.1 (2)(b)). It also became compulsory, at the appropriate 'Key Stage' in a child's schooling, to cover new 'attainment targets' for National Curriculum science which related to knowledge of how human sexual reproduction took place. The attainment targets to be covered were, and are, prescribed by Order. In relation to each of the National Curriculum subjects, details of the actual knowledge which pupils will work towards under each of the targets are set out in a separate publication. In the case of science, the relevant document is *Science in the National Curriculum* (HMSO). Amendments to the Order in August 1992 led to the inclusion of HIV/AIDS at Key Stage 3 (ages 11-14), although this topic has now been removed from National Curriculum science following the 1993 Act. Draft guidance on sex education, issued for consultation in April 1993 and intended to replace DES Circular 11/87 (op. cit.), suggested that it was 'open to the governing body to decide that no sex education should be provided...beyond that required by the National Curriculum'. However, health, including sex education, was emphasised as a 'cross-curricular' theme by the advisory body on the curriculum established under the 1988 Act, the National Curriculum Council.

It is probably true to say that, in the light of the 1988 Act and the introduction of the National Curriculum, any parent's or child's expectation that the child would receive sex education at school was justifiable, even if there was no explicit 'right' to sex education.[4]

Some parents might not have wanted their child to receive sex education at school, on principle; and some might not have approved of the particular form of sex education being offered by their child's school. In relation to the National Curriculum and, in particular, the testing of pupils, the DFEE's view has been that the duty to provide the National Curriculum overrides the general duty under section 76 of the 1944 Act (see above) to comply with parental wishes. The DFEE argues that parents who object to such testing of their children have no right to withdraw them from the tests (Harris 1993, p. 222). This interpretation seems correct. It would seem to imply that, prior to the 1993 Act, parents could have been prohibited by schools from withdrawing their children from sex education provided as part of the National Curriculum. The 1987 guidance, which pre-dated the National Curriculum, stressed that schools had a discretion over the matter and called upon them, when exercising it, to take seriously the religious and cultural objections felt by some parents towards the provision of sex education at school. After the 1988 Act, this guidance was probably relevant only to sex education provided outside the National Curriculum framework (for example, in personal and social education (PSE) classes). A subsequent draft of revised guidance (issued by the DFE in April 1993: DFE 1993a) stressed to schools the importance of taking parents' views into account in the formulation of school sex education policy, but implied that there was no scope to permit withdrawal from sex education (see para.16).

No disputes over sex education found their way into the domestic courts. Individual complaints about sex education were, however, pursued under the statutory curriculum complaints' procedure (see Education Reform Act 1988, section 23). (The complaints machinery is described in Harris 1992, including (at pp.87-91) analysis of one documented sex education complaint brought by parents of a 14-year-old girl under this procedure: (see also the complaint referred to by Robinson 1992 at 1191.) It may be noted that parents in Denmark sought to contest compulsory sex education in primary schools by arguing that it conflicted with the state's duty under the European Convention on Human Rights 1950 to provide education in accordance with parents' religious or philosophical convictions (Article 2 First Protocol). However, the Court of Human Rights gave primacy to the state's overriding duty to provide information and promote knowledge on sexual and other matters (*Kjeldsen, Busk Madsen and Pedersen v Denmark* (1976) 1 EHRR 711: see Chapter 2 by Bainham).

Parents' right to withdraw their children from religious education or collective worship continued (Education Reform Act 1988, s.9 (3)). However, until the 1993 Act (see below) they did not have a right, in furtherance of their religious or other convictions, to veto any other aspect of their children's education.

The Education Act 1993

The need for action on sex education was becoming increasingly evident by the time the various amendments to the Education Bill were before Parliament late in the Bill's passage in 1993. The case for making sex education compulsory, at least in secondary schools, was getting stronger. For example, the House of Commons Health Select Committee, in its report on *Maternity Services: Preconception* in 1990-91 (paras.70-82), highlighted the increasing problem of teenage pregnancy and perinatal mortality. It stated that it was 'concerned that health and sex education in schools may not be accorded the priority they require' (para.75). The Committee's recommendations included: incorporating sex education within the National Curriculum as a cross-curricular theme (in fact, National Curriculum Council guidance in 1990 had already advised schools on how to develop sex education in this way – see National Curriculum Council 1990a and 1990b); the designation of individual teachers as sex education co-ordinators; and national monitoring of the sex/health education curriculum.

In 1992 a survey by the Sex Education Forum, *An Enquiry into Sex Education*, found evidence that a significant number of school governing bodies, probably one-third of those in England and

Wales, did not have a written sex education policy and so were in breach of the 1986 Act. There was evidence of confusion at school level about how to include sex education in the curriculum and schools lacked the resources which would enable them to teach it. Calling for a number of improvements, including better guidance, the report stressed the importance of effective sex education at a time when an increasing proportion of young people were becoming sexually active at a younger age. The Sex Education Forum also issued guidance of its own (see Sex Education Forum 1992, *A Framework for School Sex Education*). International evidence suggested that sex education, rather than encouraging sexual activity by the young, actually postponed it (Kirby *et al.* 1994).

During the Report stage of the Education Bill in the House of Lords, Lord Stallard proposed an amendment to make it compulsory for every secondary school to provide sex education 'including the study of sexually transmitted diseases' as part of the secular curriculum, but to leave the study of any sexually transmitted disease out of the National Curriculum per se. Parents were to be given a right to withdraw their children from sex education if they had 'any strong objections on religious grounds' to it (H.L. Debs, Volume 547, columns 119-120, June 21 1993). The amendment attracted all-party support and Government assurances to return with a more tightly drafted set of provisions at a later stage. Peers agreed that teenage pregnancy and the risks from sexually-transmitted diseases made it vital to ensure that all young people received sex education. Accurate information on sexual matters was needed for young people in a society where 'everything from coffee to cars is sold through sex appeal' (*per* Lord Addington, *ibid.*, column 129).

Despite broad parliamentary support for the amendments, disquiet was expressed about the proposed ground for withdrawal: religious objection. Some of the peers who supported the right of withdrawal argued that atheists and agnostics should have it, (see, for example, Lord Renton, *ibid.*, column 135), and the Government seemed receptive to this (see Baroness Blatch, *ibid.*, column 140). Lord Addington was one of those who was opposed in principle to the right of withdrawal. He regarded 'the rights of young people – the pupils, the children – as being paramount to the rights of their parents', and he said that young people had a right to sex education (*ibid.*, column 128).

The Government's amendment was brought before the Lords at the Third Reading stage of the Bill (Volume 547, column 1290 *et seq.*, July 6 1993). The right of withdrawal from sex education was to be unconditional and not tied to any grounds: parents would be able to withdraw their children from it without having to express any reasons. Sex education would be defined in law as including information about AIDS/HIV and other sexually transmitted diseases; but references to these diseases and aspects of sexual behaviour other than 'biological aspects' would be removed from the National Curriculum. The right of withdrawal from sex education would not therefore extend to these biological aspects covered under the National Curriculum; the Minister said that 'it would be quite wrong to legislate for the possibility that some young people might leave secondary education without a clear knowledge of the basic biological and physical facts of life' (*ibid.*, column 1291). Sex education would be added to the compulsory 'basic curriculum' provided in secondary schools and for pupils receiving secondary education in special schools. The amendment was carried by 131 votes to 33 and comprises section 241 of the 1993 Act, which has made amendments to the relevant provisions of the Education Act 1944, Education (No.2) Act 1986 and Education Reform Act 1988. Draft guidance was issued in December 1993 for consultation; subsequently DFE Circular 5/94, *Education Act 1993: Sex Education in Schools* was published, in May 1994. By this time sex education had become, and remains, the subject of considerable controversy, as discussed below and in later chapters.

Compulsory sex education

In the light of the *Kjeldsen* case (*op. cit.*) there was probably no legal impediment under the European Convention on Human Rights to making sex education compulsory. The amendments made to section 18 of the Education (No.2) Act 1986 and section 2 of the Education Reform Act 1988 by the 1993 Act mean that a governing body's secular curriculum policy for a secondary school (or, in the case of a special school, for pupils receiving secondary education) cannot exclude sex education, and that sex education is now a third element in the 'basic curriculum', joining religious education and the National Curriculum (but in county, voluntary, grant-maintained and non-hospital special schools only: see s.25(1) of the 1988 Act). The position remains as before in primary schools (and where pupils receive primary education in special schools), save that where the governors' policy is that sex education should be provided, parents will, of course, now have the right to withdraw their children from it. The right of withdrawal is seen by the Government as meaning that although sex education must be provided in secondary schools, it need not be compulsory for all children.

The parental right of veto and its implications

The minister explained that

> the right of parental withdrawal is respect for the right of parents to ensure education and teaching in conformity with their own religious and philosophical convictions. This accords with Article 2 of the First Protocol of the European Convention on Human Rights. (H.L. Debs, Volume 547, column 1292, *per* Baroness Blatch.)

It was in any event seen to be desirable 'to give expression to the right of parents to play an important part in determining how their children should be educated in this particularly sensitive area of the curriculum', (*ibid.*, column 1290), hence the right of withdrawal.

The unconditional parental right to withdraw a child from sex education is contained in new section 17A of the 1988 Act. The right applies to the education of a child who is a 'pupil', which in most cases means a person aged under 19 receiving full-time education at school (see Further and Higher Education Act 1992, s.14(6)). The reason given for making the right of withdrawal unconditional, as opposed to stipulating any specific grounds, was that it was not 'appropriate or practicable to require parents to justify their request or to oblige governors to decide whether to grant these requests. If parents feel strongly enough to make such a request, that in our view is sufficient' (H.L. Debs, Volume 547, column 1291, July 6 1993, *per* Baroness Blatch).

Given the importance of effective sex education today, and the lack of any assurance that parents who withdraw their children from sex education will ensure that their children receive it at home, there is a case for demanding that acceptable reasons are provided. These could take the form of little more than a statement that the child is being withdrawn on religious grounds, but might be more specific if there are other grounds. If the parent simply dislikes the way the school teaches sex education, forcing him or her to state reasons could result in a compromise between parent and school under which some modification is made for the child concerned and the child receives sex education in school after all. This could lead on from the situation which the Department for Education's sex education Circular (DFE 1994, paragraph 36) contemplates, involving parents being invited by the school to volunteer their reasons for withdrawal 'so that any misunderstandings about the nature of sex education provided by the school can be resolved'.

A further point to bear in mind is that the law puts an obligation on each parent to ensure that their child receives an 'efficient full-time education suitable to his age, ability and aptitude and to any special educational needs he may have, whether at school or otherwise' (Education Act 1944, section 36). No general principles have emerged from the cases (see *Halsbury's Statutes*, 4th edition, Volume 15, p. 134) as to what amounts to a 'suitable' education for this purpose. However, both this section and the cases predate the 1988 Act (above). As we have seen, that Act lays down a basic curriculum which now includes sex education. Although this applies only to schools (indeed only maintained schools), the inclusion of sex education must surely be necessary if an adolescent's education is to be 'suitable'. The Department for Education's Circular on sex education (DFE 1994) implicitly acknowledges this in its advice to schools to provide assistance to parents who withdraw their children from sex education. However, this advice applies only 'where a parent wishes to discuss with the school possible ways of providing sex education at home' (para.37). In such a case the school should be 'ready to offer appropriate support, information and help, perhaps by recommending particular written materials on various aspects of sex education (including education about HIV, AIDS and other sexually transmitted diseases)' (*ibid*).

Parents may withdraw their children from *all* sex education or *any part of it*, other than the biological aspects covered under the National Curriculum. In the debates on the right of withdrawal, peers drew attention to the likely practical difficulties in its operation, in that it would often be impossible to predict in advance when sexual matters might come up for discussion at school. Yet if the right of withdrawal was to be effective, parents would have to be notified of such coverage in advance. More importantly, many peers (and, subsequently, most of the teaching unions) expressed disquiet about the fact that a person could be denied information about an activity in which he or she was lawfully entitled to participate. As Lord Addington said (H.L. Debs, Volume 547, column 1307, July 6 1993), 'when a person is over the age of 16 and is entitled to indulge in sexual activity of a heterosexual manner, surely it is absurd to the *n*th degree to deny that person information on something on which he or she can go and do the practical'. The Bishop of Guildford drew attention to the fact that at 16 a person could marry but could now be denied sex education (*ibid.*, column 1309).

Representations on the Government amendment by the Sex Education Forum, the British Medical Association and others were cited as expressing the concern that some young people would be left without vital knowledge. Peers made the point that a child withdrawn from sex education might, instead of receiving proper teaching on the subject, have to rely on 'garbled versions from their companions who have attended the class' (*ibid.,* column 1298, *per* Baroness Seear). It has to be borne in mind that survey figures show that 35 per cent of young people aged under 16 have had sexual intercourse, rising to 50 per cent of persons by the age of 18 (*ibid.,* column 1295-1296, cited by Lady Jay). Recent survey findings have also revealed that, among 16-24-year-olds, 27 per cent of boys and 17 per cent of girls have their first sexual experience before the age of 16 (Johnson and others 1994). In another survey, 32 per cent of 14-16 year olds had experienced sexual intercourse (Miller 1994, p. 27).

Attention was also focused during the passage of the 1993 Act on the lack of any rights for the children concerned. There was no provision for their views to be taken into account, despite the reference in the Children Act 1989, section 1(3) for this to be done, in the light of their age and understanding, in family proceedings on various aspects of care and upbringing. Indeed, the wishes of teenage children in particular have carried considerable weight in several important cases concerned with family disputes over a child's education and other matters (see, for example, *Re P* [1992] 1 FLR 316, which was a pre-Children Act case but one where Butler-Sloss L.J., with one eye on the forthcoming change in the law, regarded a 14-year-old's views as to the school at which he should be educated as weighty; see also *Re S* [1992] 2 FLR 313; *M v M (Minor) (Jurisdiction)* (1993) Fam. Law 396; *Re R (Child Abduction: Acquiescence)* [1995] 1 FLR 716; and *Re M (A Minor) (Child: Wishes and Feelings)* [1995] 2 FCR 90). In the U.N. Convention on the Rights of the Child 1989, article 12 states that children should be heard in all matters affecting them, 'their views being given due weight in accordance with their age and understanding'. Indeed, the Government had already acknowledged the relevance of older children's views on the quality of teaching (see Secretary of State for Education/Welsh Secretary 1992, paragraph 1.6). It had also promised that the new Code of Practice on special educational needs would 'make provision for LEAs to take into account a child's wishes and feelings, considered in the light of his or her age and understanding' (H.L. Debs, Volume 545, column 489, April 29 1993, *per* Baroness Blatch). The Code (published in May 1994) in effect requires *all* those responsible for children with special educational needs to consider their wishes in this way (DFE/Welsh Office 1994, paragraph 1.3). But the DFE's Circular on sex education (DFE 1994) says nothing on the matter other than a reference to pupil feedback in the review of sex education policies (in Annex C).

The right of parental withdrawal of a young person from sex education seems incongruous with the general acceptance (post-*Gillick*) that mature adolescents do have legal control over their own bodies; indeed those aged 16 or over are generally legally competent to give consent to medical treatment (Family Law Reform Act 1969, s. 8; see Lowe and Juss 1993). (This contradiction is discussed more fully in Bainham's chapter.) The official guidance on sex education recognises the progressive autonomy and maturity of young people as they get older. However, by giving parents but not children themselves the right of withdrawal from sex education, the legislation seems oblivious to this approach.

Most young people are opposed to the parental right to withdraw them from sex education (Burghes 1994). The 1994 guidance states that a pupil over compulsory school age who disagrees with their parent's decision on withdrawal would have to pursue the matter in the courts (see DFE 1994, paragraph 36). This would involve the pupil seeking a Children Act 1989 section 8 order ('specific issue') (see Chapter 2). It seems that one teaching union, the Association of Teachers and Lecturers, is prepared to support children who want to take such legal action where their parents seek to prevent them from receiving sex education at school ('Union backs pupils denied sex facts', *Times Educational Supplement* March 11, 1994).

Disputes are also possible between different persons with a claim to be able to exercise parental responsibility in respect of the child, given that the Education Acts now define 'parent' as including not only parents and guardians but also 'any person … who is not a parent but who has responsibility for him … or who has care of him' (Education Act 1944, s. 114(1D); for discussion see Piper 1994). In the case of a request for withdrawal of a child from sex education, there could be a conflict between the 'parents' which school will probably have to resolve in favour of the person making the request, unless and until a parent who opposes the withdrawal secures a court order (probably a 'prohibited steps' order under section 8 of the Children Act 1989: these orders are discussed by Bainham in Chapter 2). (For an attempt by a divorced parent to obtain a 'prohibited steps' order to stop the parent with residence sending the child to a boarding school, see *Re G (Parental Responsibility: Education)* [1995] 2 FCR 53). This is a problem which the DFE's Circular on sex education (5/94 *op. cit.*) largely ignores. It states merely that the right of withdrawal may be made by 'either parent or a person who has responsibility of care of the child' (para.36). Some schools may be unaware that an unmarried father will not, unless he has acquired parental responsibility by agreement or order under the Children Act 1989, have the right of withdrawal under new section 17A of the 1988 Act, whereas a divorced father living away from the family will enjoy this right.

One contention, put forward by Lord Judd in the House of Lords, about the right of withdrawal is that it could give rise to a denial of the child's right to education guaranteed by the European Convention on Human Rights 1950 (Article 2, First Protocol; see the U.N. Convention on the Rights of the Child 1989, below). The Government has denied that this is the case, while refusing to reveal its source of legal advice (H.L. Debs, Volume 547, column 1321, July 6 1993). The difficulty with the denial argument is that the Convention and other international treaty obligations (for example, the International Covenant on Economic, Social and Cultural Rights 1966) do not specify any basic content of 'education' – they only call on states to ensure that education respects parents' or guardians' moral, philosophical or religious convictions and upholds human dignity (Feldman 1993, p. 888). The U.N. Convention on the Rights of the Child 1989 also requires primary education to be compulsory and free and requires secondary education to take different forms, including general and vocational (see article 28). The fact that the European Court of Human Rights was prepared in *Kjeldsen* (*op. cit.*) to hold that a state policy of compulsory sex education could override parental convictions irrespective of the duty to ensure conformity to them should probably not be taken to imply that the right to education encompasses a right to sex education. The provision of sex education or its exclusion from the curriculum are clearly seen as matters within the power and competence of an individual state to determine. This issue is considered further by Bainham in Chapter 2.

A further issue was raised by the NSPCC in its comments on the unconditional right of withdrawal. It argued that parents who had been subjecting their children to sexual abuse might exercise their right of withdrawal to prevent their activities being exposed through discussion of sexual matters (see H.L. Debs, Volume 547, column 1295, July 6 1993). This is a strong argument and one that has not been answered by the Government.

As we have seen, there are important points of principle arising out of the parental right of withdrawal of a child from sex education at school. There are also key practical issues to be resolved, such as whether parents must be given advance warning of sexual content and how disputes between parents as to the exercise of the right of withdrawal are to be handled. It should be borne in mind, however, that withdrawal is not expected to occur on a wide scale. In one survey only four per cent of parents felt that schools should not provide sex education (Allen 1987, p. 177). In a more recent survey less than three per cent of parents felt that schools should not play a part in educating children about sexuality and their own sexual development (NFER 1994).

The content of sex education

The general approach

Inevitably a link has been made between the content of sex education at school and the parental right to withdraw a child from it. Reports – some exaggerated – about the explicit and salacious nature of some sex education classes and literature have fuelled arguments about the primacy of the moral right of parents to play a protective role in guiding their children's social development. (See, for example, the correspondence generated by the Family Planning Association's published materials on primary school sex education: *The Times*, October 30, 1993.) One report concerned alleged explicit discussion of particular sexual practices by a school nurse – 'Sex lessons nurse "shattered"', *The Times*, March 25, 1994 – whilst controversial literature has included the Health Education Authority-commissioned leaflet *Your Pocket Guide to Sex*, which was withdrawn by the Authority in March 1994 after Government intervention and claims that it was 'smutty' (see 'Author defends sex book as informative', *The Times*, March 25, 1994, and 'Tory right halt sex education campaigns', *Independent on Sunday*, April 17, 1994; see also 'Archbishop bans Catholic sex guide for schools', *The Times* October 23, 1994).

But for the most part this moral right, reinforced by a legal right under the amendment made by section 241 of the 1993 Act, has been promoted independently of any explicit general disapproval of sex education as provided by schools in England and Wales. As Viscount Caldecote said in the debate on the Government's amendment to the Education Bill in 1993, 'if in carrying out their parental duty...parents believe that the education being given is unsuitable in relation to their child, then caring and loving parents will want to remove their child and provide the education themselves' (H.L. Debs, Volume 547, column 1307, July 6 1993). From the 1987 Circular (DES 1987) onwards, the Government has stressed the need for sex education to be approached with sensitivity to the wishes and beliefs of particular cultural and religious groups, who may have strong feelings on the subject. This approach, it has been stressed, has extended not only to permitting parents to withdraw their children from sex education (under pre-1993 Act voluntary arrangements), but also to working in partnership with parents in the development of school sex education policies.

The law's prescription of the content of sex education has involved the requirement, discussed above, concerning the taking of steps by LEAs, governing bodies and head teachers to ensure that sex education is given in such a manner as to encourage pupils 'to have due regard to moral considerations and the value of family life' (Education (No.2) Act 1986, s.46). Also, sex education has been included within the attainment targets for science under the National Curriculum and (as part of health education), again noted above. However, section 241 requires the Secretary of State to remove aspects of sex education (other than biological aspects) from National Curriculum science, using for this purpose his power to prescribe the attainment targets, programmes of study, and so on, for each subject under section 4 of the Education Reform Act 1988. This power has now been exercised. Schools' requirement to cover HIV/AIDS and to ensure that pupils 'understand the need to have a responsible attitude to sexual behaviour' at Key Stage 3 (see above) has been deleted (Education (National Curriculum) (Attainment Targets and Programmes of Study in Science) (Amendment) Order 1994 SI 1994 No.1520).

As regards sex education in *primary* schools, the 1987 guidance stressed that at this level sex education should 'aim to help pupils cope with the physical and emotional challenges of growing up and give them an elementary understanding of human reproduction'. This predated the 1988 Act (see s.1(2)) which, as noted above, requires schools to prepare pupils for the experiences and responsibilities of adult life, but was not felt to require revision in the light of this change to the legal framework. Indeed it was replicated exactly in the DFE's draft sex education circular (subsequently withdrawn) which was issued in April 1993. The present circular (DFE 1994) also contains it (para.10), but new, sensible, preliminary guidance is also offered. It explains that 'very great care should be taken to match any sex education provided to the maturity of the pupils involved, which may not always correspond to their chronological age'. Government plans to advise schools about organising sex education classes by 'streaming' them according to pupils' individual maturity and knowledge of sexual matters were heavily criticised (with regard, in particular, to the practical difficulties of ascertaining individuals' degree of knowledge) and were dropped (see 'Unions condemn streaming of sex education' *The Times*, May 2, 1994). Instead, the Circular advises that sex education 'should be geared to the needs of the class or group as a whole, and should not be determined by the pace of the most precocious pupils whose needs can be met in other ways' (reference is made to another part of the guidance, dealing with one-to-one advice with parental approval).

At *secondary* level, the advice in the 1987 Circular to include education about sexually transmitted diseases continues in the 1994 Circular (DFE 1994, paragraph 11) but is now a legal requirement in any event. The moral dimension and the reference to the promotion of stable family life, required under the 1986 Act (see above), continue to be stressed.

Homosexuality

There was no attempt in the 1987 Circular to proscribe coverage of homosexuality in sex education, but schools were advised that among some religious faiths such coverage could cause 'deep offence' (para.22). They were also advised that 'there is no place in any school in any circumstances for teaching which advocates homosexual behaviour, which presents it as the norm, or which encourages homosexual experimentation by pupils'. There is no corresponding guidance in the 1994 Circular. Given the parental right of withdrawal of a child from sex education, it could be argued that there is less pressure on teachers to omit information on homosexuality from sex education, provided parents are warned about this in advance. There is, of course, a strong case for inclusion of homosexuality in sex education to ensure that the educational needs of young homosexuals are properly catered for, especially following the reduction in the age of consent for male homosexual acts. This is discussed further in Chapter 4 by Lois Bibbings.

Children with special educational needs

There is separate guidance in the 1994 Circular on sex education in special schools (that is, schools specifically geared to the needs of those with learning difficulties, including those with behavioural disorders). Although there are no special requirements concerning sex education for people with learning difficulties attending ordinary schools, the general principle is that wherever possible such children should engage 'in the activities of the school together with children who do not have special educational needs' (Education Act 1993, section 161(4)). (On sex education for people with learning difficulties, see Craft 1987 and 1993.) It should be noted, however, that this general integration duty does not apply where, amongst other things, the child's education would be prejudiced by his/her being educated alongside children who do not have learning difficulties under the 1993 Act. Given the importance of sex education, there will sometimes be a case for providing it on a one-to-one or small group basis to a child with special educational needs. This will in most cases be a matter for decision by the school's special educational needs co-ordinator (SENCO), acting in accordance with the Code of Practice under Part III of the Act (DFE/Welsh Office 1994).

Conclusion

The law now regulates the provision and content of sex education in a number of ways. If it is complied with, few children should leave school with inadequate knowledge of contraception and guidance as to sexual behaviour, although there will continue to be debate about the more controversial areas such as the way that homosexuality is treated. The actual extent, in practice, of teachers' remaining autonomy with regard to sex education is yet to be ascertained. The provision of contraceptive advice by teachers is not covered by the recent legislative changes, and the 1994 guidance (in DFE Circular 5/94) merely creates uncertainty. However, expert opinion considers that teachers will not generally incur liability for giving such advice if acting in the best interests of the child (see Chapters 2 and 3 by Bainham and Bridgeman respectively).

Sex education is generally part of the *secular* curriculum of a school, but the right of withdrawal, although not tied to any grounds, may be expected to be exercised primarily on the grounds of *religious* belief (see Chapter 5 by Bradney). In some nation states the Constitution guarantees religious neutrality in schools, as opposed to a mere statement of respect for all religions and beliefs, as in France (see Bell 1990) and The Netherlands (see article 23 of the Dutch Constitution). Such a guarantee is offered by the First Amendment to the U.S. Constitution, which prohibits state 'establishment' of religion (the 'Establishment Clause'). Thus U.S. parents have had an opportunity, not available to parents in

England and Wales, to argue before the courts that any provision of sex education or sexual content in other subjects (principally literature) which conflicts with their religious beliefs could be unconstitutional. Whitson (1992, p. 60) notes, however, how the U.S. courts' response to these claims has been 'generally…to support state and local school authorities in cases dealing with sex education programs'. In *Smith* v *Ricci* 459 U.S. 962 (1982), for example, the Supreme Court of New Jersey rejected arguments that, *inter alia*, a family life education programme which included sex education infringed the Establishment Clause, partly on the basis that parents who objected had a right under the relevant state regulation to withdraw their children from the programme.

The introduction of more compulsory health and sex education in the U.S. in response to rising public concern about AIDS has precipitated an increase in legal disputes. In one case a New York State appeals court held that the application of a state regulation compelling the provision of AIDS education at school could be not be dis-applied on the basis of religious objection, because of the 'substantial and compelling State interest' in preventing AIDS transmission (*Ware v Valley Stream H.S. Dist* (1989) 545 N.Y.S. 2d at 320, cited by Whitson *op. cit.* at p. 61). Whitson (*op. cit.*) concludes that the cases in the U.S. demonstrate that

> the inclusion of sex education in the elementary and secondary school curriculum will generally be treated as something to be politically determined as a matter of legislative policy, and not as a constitutional matter on which courts would overrule decisions by the state or local legislative and administrative bodies.

(In the U.S. the curriculum is regulated by state rather than federal legislation (see Yudof 1982).)

The law in England and Wales puts the provision of sex education under the same degree of legislative control but gives parents an unconditional right of choice over whether their child receives it. This means that disputes are more likely to focus on the content of sex education. Media interest in sex education stories and schools' consequent sensitivity and caution make it easier for determined parents to influence the policy and approach followed in schools in a way that obviously goes beyond the basic right of withdrawal.

Notes

1. The Department for Education and Department of Employment were merged in July 1995 to form the Department for

Education and Employment (DFEE). It was announced that Lord Henley would have ministerial responsibility for the school curriculum: DFEE Press Release 147/95, July 11 1995.

2. As Kirby (1995, p. 403) says, although schools are well placed to provide education on sexual matters, 'conditions in schools may not be ideal: class time is limited, teachers are often not trained in handling sensitive subjects, and considerable controversy surrounds the teaching of some subjects'.
3. See, for example, *Watt v Kesteven C.C.* [1955] 1 All ER 473; *Cumings v Birkenhead Corporation* [1972] Ch. 12; see further Harris (1993), pp. 120-122 and 130-132.
4. On the right to education in general, see Harris (1990) and Feldman (1993), Chapter 18.4.

2. Sex education: a family lawyer's perspective

Andrew Bainham, Fellow of Christ's College, Cambridge and Lecturer in Law, The University of Cambridge

Introduction

The question of the availability and content of sex education in schools is just one aspect of a much wider debate about children's rights, the rights and responsibilities of parents and the role of the state in family life. My purpose here is to offer the perspective of a family lawyer and to examine the contribution that the wider principles of family law might make to the resolution of educational issues generally and sex education in particular.

The starting point must be that there can be a conflict of interest between parents and children in the sphere of education. This might be presented as a clash of their respective 'rights' or, equally valid in my view, a clash between children's 'rights' and parents' 'responsibilities' or between their respective 'interests'. The precise terminology chosen is not perhaps as important as the acknowledgement that these conflicts can exist[1] or the basis upon which they are resolved. Many examples could be taken from family law to illustrate the possible conflict of interest between parents and children. We might point to the separate representation of children in care and related proceedings[2] or to the intervention of the courts to authorise life-saving surgery for children in the face of parental opposition, often on religious grounds (see, for example, *Re S (A Minor) (Medical Treatment)* [1993] 2 FLR 376 and *Re O (A Minor) (Medical Treatment)* [1993] 2 FLR 149). It is not, I believe, difficult to postulate a conflict of interest between parent and child over sex education. The religious fundamentalist might, for example, wish to prevent his child's exposure to 'value-free' sex education which might impart information in a neutral way about contraceptives, 'safer sex' and sexually transmitted diseases. Yet, on the child's behalf it might be urged that such information is necessary to protect both the child and others. To take another case, it was suggested in the House of Lords during the debates on the Education Bill 1993 that a sexual abuser might not welcome the enlightenment of his child in sexual matters and might seek to exercise the newly-created right of parental withdrawal to cover up his own illegitimate activities.[3] This is an extreme, some would say unrealistic, scenario but it does demonstrate rather well that the interests of parents and children in this matter cannot be regarded as synonymous.

I begin by looking at the developing concept of children's rights and the distinctly English notion of parental responsibility enshrined in the Children Act 1989. I focus, where appropriate, on their application in an educational context. I then consider the position of children and parents under the United Nations Convention on the Rights of the Child and the European Convention on Human Rights. In the next section I seek to apply these broader principles of family law to sex education and I examine the two issues which have given rise to the greatest controversy – the parental right of withdrawal and advice or counselling on sexual matters given by teachers to individual pupils. I conclude with a few general observations about the current state of sex education law, its consistency with the wider principles of family law and its compatibility with the U.K.'s obligations as a member of the international community.

Children's rights

The expression 'children's rights', has been described as 'a slogan in search of a definition' (Rodham 1973, p.487). There are many different interpretations of the idea. Yet I think there is broad agreement that the concept of children's rights must at least embrace a protective or paternalistic element together with an element of autonomy or self-determination which becomes more significant as the child gets older. Many of the theories of children's rights have been concerned with this balance between paternalism and self-determination.[4] One of the most useful categorisations of the rights which children might plausibly claim was put forward by Michael Freeman in 1983. He suggested four broad categories: rights to welfare; rights of protection; the right to be treated like adults; and rights against parents. What I think is interesting about sex education is that it would appear to span all of these categories. It clearly falls within the notion of welfare rights which is wide enough to include the provision of *positive benefits* or rights of *recipience* as distinguished from rights of *protection* which are essentially *negative* in that their aim is to prevent *harm* to the child. Yet sex education can also be brought within this latter category since its role in protecting the child from unwanted pregnancy and sexually transmitted diseases surely cannot be doubted. Freeman's third and fourth categories are concerned with the self-determination aspect of rights. Together they embrace the idea that as fellow human beings children should be treated like adults unless there is a good reason for treating them differently and that they should enjoy a measure of independence from parental control commensurate with their age and maturity. Again I think that sex education can be seen to fall within this species of rights. It can be argued that children are entitled to decide for themselves that they wish to acquire appropriate knowledge about sexual matters in order to prepare themselves for adulthood.

An alternative way of looking at things would be to abandon 'rights-talk' altogether and to concentrate instead on the underlying *interests* which children may be thought to have. This is essentially the approach of John Eekelaar (1986a) who, in his theory of children's rights, distinguishes between three broad interests which children may claim – 'basic interests', 'developmental interests' and the 'autonomy interest'. If we were to adopt this approach I think we would be driven to much the same conclusion that sex education traverses all the relevant categories. It is a 'basic interest' because it is concerned with protecting the child's essential health and well-being; it is a 'developmental interest' since it is at least partly concerned with ensuring the healthy development of the child and, to paraphrase Eekelaar, minimising the degree to which the child enters adult life affected by avoidable prejudices incurred during childhood. Finally, it again falls within the 'autonomy interest' which implies the child's 'freedom to choose his own lifestyle and to enter social relations according to his own inclinations uncontrolled by the authority of the adult world, whether parents or institutions' (Eekelaar 1986a, p.171).

What this analysis should demonstrate is that to see sex education purely as a matter of the child's choice or autonomy would be an unbalanced and one-dimensional view. A case can certainly be made for saying that the 'Gillick-competent' (*Gillick v West Norfolk and Wisbech Area Health Authority* [1986] 1 A.C. 112) child has in principle the right to provide the necessary *consent* to receive sex education in the face of parental objection (but not apparently the right to *object* to receiving it: see below) and the spirit if not the letter, of the Children Act 1989[5] certainly requires that in the event of a dispute the views of the child should be given proper consideration. However, as a matter of strict law, I will argue that *Gillick* cannot override the statutory right of parental withdrawal conferred by the Education Act 1993 (s.241(3), inserting a new section 17A into the Education Reform Act 1988). But to dwell on these technicalities is to miss the point. The key argument I wish to present is that the right to sex education, at least on a theoretical level, is a multidimensional right which is not confined to the autonomy claim. Indeed I have elsewhere criticised the unhelpful, but prevalent, trend in England to treat as synonymous the *general* notion of children's rights and the *particular* right or interest in autonomy.

Let me illustrate my point. Suppose that the child happens to agree with his parents, perhaps for religious reasons, that he should receive no sex education and should be withdrawn from classes. This would be an exercise of autonomy (although there could be an issue as to undue influence by the parent); but would it also secure his rights or protect his interests? It is at least arguable that to perpetuate a situation of ignorance in an area so crucial to the child's development would *not* be in his interests and would therefore be contrary to his rights. In other words, the paternalism of the state in compelling him to receive some sex education could be justified and could override *both* his views and those of his parents. Lest this be thought too radical we should I think remind ourselves that as a society we are prepared to do exactly this by the very creation of a compulsory education system and the provision of a national curriculum. The law does not *generally* allow parents or children to decide that the children should receive *no* education[6] and the *content* of that education is these days heavily prescriptive.

A useful analogy might also be drawn here with the medical arena where in recent years the courts have shown a willingness to intervene paternalistically to protect children from the objective harm to which their own decisions might expose them. (The most significant decisions are *Re R (A Minor) (Wardship: Consent to Treatment)* [1992] Fam. 11 and *Re W (A Minor) (Medical Treatment: Court's Jurisdiction)* [1992] 3 WLR 758.) A particularly striking example of this was the decision of Ward J. to override the continued opposition of a 15-year-old and his parents (all three being Jehovah's Witnesses) to a blood transfusion necessary to save his life (*Re E (A Minor) (Wardship: Medical Treatment)* [1993] 1 FLR 386).

I do not think therefore that the child's right to sex education rests exclusively, or even primarily, on his capacity to consent to its provision and I agree with those who in the parliamentary debates on the Education Bill regarded the application of any such test of maturity in this context as inappropriate and unworkable (see particularly Baroness Blatch, H.L. Debs, 6 July 1993, col. 1293). I hope I have rather succeeded in demonstrating that the right we are talking about is a good deal more sophisticated than this.

Parents' rights and responsibilities

It is almost heresy these days for family lawyers to talk of parental 'rights'. A primary purpose of the Children Act 1989 was to get away from the whole notion of children as possessions over which parents had some sort of proprietary claim. Hence the Act changed the terminology – parents were no longer to have 'rights' as such but 'parental responsibility', an all-embracing idea which, confusingly, includes any parental 'rights' which may have survived the reforms (s.3(1))! The Scots have taken a different line and consider it appropriate to continue to distinguish between parents' rights and responsibilities (Scottish Law Commission 1992).

Another way of looking at this matter is, as in the case of children, to look at parents' 'interests' as opposed to rights. The focus of attention here has been on whether it is legitimate to recognise an *independent* parental interest which exists other than to promote the welfare of the child. While it is not exactly in vogue to assert that there is, I am personally convinced by the rather compelling argument of McCall Smith (1990). The argument states that if we concentrate on the *beneficiary* of parental actions taken in relation to children, it is quite possible to conceive of situations in which that beneficiary is the *parent* and not the child. McCall Smith thus postulates the existence of two categories of parental rights, namely 'parent-centred parental rights' and 'child-centred parental rights'. However we conceptualise the parental position, the undeniable fact, noted above, is that there may be a clash between what the parent wants and what the child wants or needs and it is the role of the law to resolve this conflict. The chief difficulty with which English (and I think Scottish) law is having to grapple is precisely how the notion of children's rights, especially rights of decision-making, can be reconciled and can co-exist with the legal responsibility of parents which undeniably lasts until children attain majority.[7] Attempts by the courts to resolve this dilemma have in some ways only served to obscure the issue further. But where we appear to stand at the moment, at least in relation to medical decision-making, is that a mature child with the requisite understanding (for what is required of the child, see particularly the speech of Lord Scarman in *Gillick*, above) seems to have the legal capacity to give a *consent* which would empower a third party to deal with him or her and would obviate the necessity for parental consent (*ibid*). Conversely, such a child does *not* have the capacity to *object* to such dealings if the parent (or other person with parental responsibility) is prepared to provide the third party with the necessary consent. These principles have been fashioned in the medical context and there must be some doubt about how far they can be extrapolated to the educational sphere. The position we have arrived at may also be criticised as illogical but it does serve to illuminate one matter which I regard as relevant to the sex education debate. The important point is this. The Court of Appeal decisions (*Re R* and *Re W* above) have emphasised that the function of consent in the medical context is to prevent actions by the medical profession from being tortious. It is for that reason that *either* the child's consent *or* the parent's will do. (Consent, to borrow the imagery of Lord Donaldson MR in the above cases, operates as a key which unlocks a door (*Re R*) or as a legal flackjacket (*Re W*).) Now, if we apply this to education, and specifically to the question of advice and counselling given by teachers to pupils, a question which must be addressed is precisely *why* it is alleged that parental consent would be required. What tort or other unlawful act would be committed in the course of advice-giving or counselling in the absence of parental consent and why would the child's consent in this context not be good enough? I address this issue below.

Before leaving the general question of parental responsibility we should pause to reflect briefly on something which is, in my view, frequently neglected or ignored in the analysis of the parent's position. This is the matter of criminal responsibility for abuse or neglect. The principal provision is still section 1 of the Children and Young Persons Act 1933, which makes it an offence for anyone over 16 with 'responsibility' for a child, *inter alia*, to neglect a child 'in a manner likely to cause him unnecessary suffering or injury to health' (s.1(1)). For these purposes the requisite neglect may be established by failure to provide medical aid (s.1(2)(a)). We heard nothing of this provision in the *Gillick* saga during which it was alleged that a parent had an absolute right to veto the provision of contraceptive advice or treatment for minors. And we have heard nothing of it during the current debate about whether a parent has an absolute right to deny sex education to his or her child. I am not suggesting for a moment that a parent would be liable to prosecution for withholding these things from a sexually active child, but what I would argue is this. The very existence of the offence is public recognition of the basic duties which parents have to protect the health and well-being of their minor children. The spirit of this legislation suggests that parents should consider very carefully how far they should seek to discourage sexual activity by effectively increasing the hazards attendant upon it.[8]

Let me now turn briefly to the parents' position in education law. I have commented elsewhere that

> no student of children law, looking at education, can fail to be struck by the contrast between the emphasis on parents' *rights* in education alongside the movement from rights to *responsibilities* elsewhere in the law (Bainham 1993, Chapter 16).

The inhibitions of the family lawyer to talk of parental rights have certainly not been shared by the Government in formulating its education policy nor are they reflected in the education legislation. We have, for example, the *parents'* charter (a revised version of which was published in 1994), *parental* choice of school (Education Act 1980; for a full discussion see Harris 1993, Chapter 5), *parent* governors (but not, be it noted, pupil governors – not under this administration anyway[9]) and the *parental* right of withdrawal from religious education and collective worship.[10] It seems only natural that we should now be talking about the *parent's* 'absolute right' to withdraw his or her child from sex education. But is it really so natural? Why are we prepared in the educational context to attach such precedence to the parents' position when we are not prepared to do so on any other aspect of upbringing? And just what has happened to the rights of *children* at school? I suggest that the effect of the domestic educational policy of recent years has been to eclipse children's rights in stark contrast to the eclipse of parental rights elsewhere (I borrow the phrase from John Eekelaar 1986b). It seems that if we wish to assert rights in education for children it is to the international community that we must now turn.

The international dimension

The child's right to education is explicitly recognised in a number of international conventions. The two most significant for our purposes are the United Nations Convention on the Rights of the

Child[11] and the European Convention on Human Rights.[12] There are however several difficulties which would have to be faced if we wanted to argue that these Conventions created a right to sex education which could not be overridden by parental objection.

The first difficulty is that the right to education is couched in broad and general terms in each Convention and neither makes explicit reference to sex education. 'Education' lacks detailed definition and any such right could arise only by implication. However it is certainly arguable in the case of the UN Convention that the right to education in Article 28, when read with the fundamental aims of education set out in Article 29, does create a *prima facie* right to sex education. These include, amongst other things, 'the development of the child's personality, talents, mental and physical abilities to their fullest potential' (Article 29(1)(a)) and 'the preparation of the child for responsible life in a free society' (Article 29(1)(d)).

The second difficulty is that even if the child does have a *prima facie* right to sex education, this is qualified by the state's obligation to show proper respect for the role of parents. This is recognised in more than one article of the UN Convention. Thus, Article 5 requires States' Parties to

> respect the responsibilities, rights and duties of parents...to provide, in a manner consistent with the evolving capacities of the child, appropriate direction and guidance in the exercise by the child of the rights recognised in the present Convention (see also Article 14(2)).

Does this perhaps mean that the child's right to sex education, if it exists at all, is a *qualified* rather than an absolute right?

The issue of sex education came before the European Court as long ago as 1976 in *Kjeldsen, Busk Madsen and Pedersen v. Denmark* (7 December 1976, Series A No.23). There is no doubt that the decision fell short of recognising the child's right to sex education.[13] Indeed, the focus of attention was not on the rights of children under the Convention but on the rights of their parents. The dispute arose out of Danish legislation which introduced compulsory, integrated sex education and which had the effect of removing the existing rights of parents to exempt their children from sex education. They alleged that the scheme was contrary to the beliefs which they held as Christians and, as such, violated their rights under Article 2, First Protocol. This provides: 'In the exercise of any functions which it assumes in relation to education and to teaching, the state shall respect the right of parents to ensure such education and teaching is in conformity with their own religious and philosophical convictions'. The Court took the view that the Danish scheme conveyed sex education in an objective, critical and pluralistic manner and did not amount to any attempt on the part of the state to indoctrinate children. It decided that it was open to the state to introduce a compulsory scheme which presented sex education in this balanced and objective manner. It did *not* decide that the child had a right which *required* the state to introduce such a scheme. Neither did it decide that no scheme of compulsory sex education could breach the parental rights enshrined in the Convention. It may well be that the Court might now be persuaded (especially in the light of the more detailed rights to education contained in the UN Convention) that the child *does* have a right which requires the introduction of a compulsory scheme with no right of parental withdrawal, but it has not yet addressed this issue. Again, it might accept that a blanket right of withdrawal pays too much respect to parental rights under the Convention, but it has not yet addressed this issue either.

The final difficulty in relying on international law is that the rights under the Conventions are extremely difficult to enforce. There is no direct legal mechanism for enforcing the rights in the UN Convention, which is more a matter of political accountability (the role of the Committee on the Rights of the Child, established under Article 43, is important in this respect). Petitions can be brought by or on behalf of children under the European Convention but the process is lengthy and cumbersome since the Convention is not directly incorporated into English law. (The foundation of such a petition could be Article 2, First Protocol which enshrines the right to education. An alternative could be Article 8, which protects an individual's private and family life from state interference, or Article 10, which includes, *inter alia*, the right to receive information and ideas without interference by public authority.) The child would need to be represented by a guardian *ad litem* who for obvious reasons could not be the parent (unless of course the dispute involved a disagreement between the two parents themselves. I address this issue in the context of section 8 orders below). Moreover, the child would first have to exhaust domestic remedies which, for these purposes, would be primarily the procedures under the Children Act 1989 which I consider below. The fact is that, while the European Convention is not for adults alone, almost all the cases concerning children which have been decided under it have been brought by parents, and have been concerned with parents' rights under the Convention and how far the state may legitimately interfere with their exercise. Nonetheless, the principles in these Conventions provide an important benchmark against which the substance of domestic law may be evaluated.

Sex education and the family

Sex education in schools is now governed by section 241 of the Education Act 1993, which amends the Education Reform Act 1988. The salient features of the new law, set out more fully in Chapter 1 by Neville Harris, are as follows. Sex education became compulsory and part of the 'basic' curriculum in all maintained schools as from 1 September 1994. At the same time, everything except the biological aspects (viz. the biology of human sexual development and reproduction) were removed from the National Curriculum. In particular, it was expressly provided that the subject of Science in the National Curriculum should be revised to *exclude* knowledge of AIDS, HIV, other sexually transmitted diseases and aspects of human sexual behaviour other than the biological aspects (s.241(4)). A parent was given, for the first time, an *absolute* right to withdraw his or her child, wholly or partly, from sex education, except in so far as it is comprised in the National Curriculum (s.241(3)). The parent is not required to give reasons and the right of withdrawal applies to all pupils, including those above the school-leaving age and (in the case of girls) the age of consent for sexual activity (under section 241(1) the new provisions apply to 'all registered pupils'). These provisions apply to maintained secondary schools. In relation to primary schools, sex education will, as before the Act, be the responsibility of governors to decide whether to offer it and to determine its manner and content. Where parents do not wish their child to receive some or all of that on offer they may exercise their right of withdrawal (see Baroness Blatch, H.L. Debs, 6 July 1993 cols 1290-1291). It should finally be noted that the reforms have not affected the general principle introduced by section 46 of the Education (No. 2) Act 1986 which requires that all sex education offered in schools be given 'with due regard to moral considerations and the value of family life'.

The new law has generated considerable controversy and I will offer the view of a family lawyer on what are probably the two most disputed issues. These are:

1. What is the legal position if the child should disagree with his or her parents who are purporting to exercise their statutory right to withdraw him or her from sex education? In fact there is a further question here which immediately occurs to the

family lawyer. What is the position where the two parents themselves disagree? One wishes to withdraw the child and the other does not.

2. What is the legal position where a teacher is approached by a pupil who has been withdrawn from sex education and the teacher is minded to offer the pupil advice or counselling about such matters as contraception, abortion or other sexually-related questions?

The right of withdrawal – resolving disputes in the family

The 1993 Act appears then to give to the parent an absolute right to withdraw his or her child from sex education. Yet, as noted above, as a general proposition the child who has achieved 'Gillick competence' has a right to take decisions for him/herself. The assessment of the child's competence falls on the third party dealing with the child.[14] In this case it would be the school, subject only to the possibility of a subsequent challenge in the courts. On the other hand it seems also to be established that even a competent child does not have the right to *object* to something which is authorised by a parent (*Re R* and *Re W* above). I think we can dispose of this latter scenario fairly quickly. As the law stands there would appear to be no basis upon which the child him/herself could refuse to receive sex education where the parents are in favour of it and do not wish to exercise their right of withdrawal.

Let me then return to the more difficult case of the willing child and the objecting parent. How are we to reconcile what looks like an unqualified right of the parent with what appears to be decision-making capacity on the part of the child? I think the answer in law, however difficult to justify on a theoretical or philosophical level, is straightforward. *Gillick* is about the *common law* and was never intended to apply in situations where the particular issue was governed by *statute*.[15] It was recognised in the case itself that it was open to Parliament to determine that children should, or should not, have capacity to take specific decisions. Common law principles should resolve only those issues not directly governed by statute.[16] Game, set and match to the parent – but is it?

The matter is further complicated in that, under general principles of family law, the courts have long exercised their jurisdiction to override the wishes of parents where they claim this is necessary to protect the best interests of a child. Traditionally wardship has been used for these purposes but it is likely that such a dispute would now be more appropriately resolved by a 'section 8 order' under the Children Act 1989. A 'specific issue order' is an order 'giving directions for the purpose of determining a specific question which has arisen, or which may arise, in connection with any aspect of parental responsibility for a child'. Clearly educational questions fall within this definition. An alternative might be a 'prohibited steps order', being an order 'that no step which could be taken by a parent in meeting his parental responsibility for a child, and which is of a kind specified in the order, shall be taken by any person without the consent of the court'. This order might conceivably be sought by a parent wishing to prevent a school from discussing sexual matters with a child contrary to his or her wishes.

The scheme of the 1989 Act is that parents or others with residence orders (and thus parental responsibility) may apply for a section 8 order as of right (s.10(4)). Others require the leave of the court and, in the case of adult applicants, the legislation specifies the criteria the court must take into account (s.10(1) and (9)). The application may also be brought by the child him/herself. The child also requires leave which can only be granted where the court 'is satisfied that he has sufficient understanding to make the proposed application for the S8 order' (s.10(8)). If this were the end of the matter one could be reasonably confident that a child who bothered to take a dispute with parents this far would be judged by the court in that case to have the requisite level of understanding. But the early signs are that the courts are likely to be less than enthusiastic about entertaining applications by children and are likely to refuse leave unless they regard the issue as a sufficiently 'serious' matter. It has been held that only questions of a certain level of seriousness were within the contemplation of Parliament in opening the courts to children (*Re C (A Minor) (Leave to Seek Section 8 Order)* [1994] 1 FLR 26). This approach reserves to the courts a large residual discretion to accept jurisdiction or refuse to adjudicate on parent-child disputes; but the courts have not been wholly consistent thus far. Another decision[17] suggests a more liberal approach. This would be to accept jurisdiction where the child has the requisite level of understanding and to refuse leave only in those cases which patently have no hope of success on the merits.

Assuming the court is prepared to exercise jurisdiction, what is the likely result? It is of course axiomatic that the welfare principle will govern the matter[18] and that this will turn on an assessment of the individual child's best interests within the overall context of the family situation. It should also be borne in mind that the courts are now enjoined *not* to make any order unless they consider that 'doing so would be better for the child than making no order at all' (Children Act 1989, s.1(5)). The effect of this provision should not be underestimated. There is already one reported example of a court taking the view that, notwithstanding an unresolved dispute between an adolescent and her parents, it would be better for the family to resolve the dispute internally rather than for the court to intervene (*Re SC* – see n.17). Even if the child applicant were able to overcome these hurdles, there must be a serious chance that the court would be reluctant to interfere with what appears to be an absolute statutory right of withdrawal. We have seen that generally the parental position is not conceived in such absolute terms and that, on other questions, the court might be rather more willing to interfere with the exercise of parental responsibility.

None of this is very encouraging from the child's point of view but I think there are two sets of circumstances in which the court *would* be more likely to intervene on the side of the child. The first is where the dispute is not child versus united parents but child and one parent versus the other parent. In some ways this is a more realistic scenario. We should especially bear in mind the high rate of separation and divorce and the fact that both divorced parents now retain full parental responsibility for the child (Children Act 1989, s.2). It is entirely conceivable that the 'absent' parent[19] will disagree with the 'residential' parent about issues of upbringing. Education is perhaps the most obvious of these since it accounts for such a large part of the child's life. It would be tempting to say that the court would be likely to support the parent actually looking after the child on a daily basis. But this cannot be regarded as a foregone conclusion for several reasons. First, the welfare principle applies and the courts have long accepted that in some circumstances the view of the 'absent' parent should prevail where this accords more with the child's best interests.[20] Secondly, the theory of the Children Act is quite clear that no premium attaches to the parental responsibility of the residential parent. Apart from the question of where the child is to live, a residence order does not upset the equilibrium of parental responsibility. Thirdly, and perhaps most significantly, the court is likely to support the *combined* view of an older child and one parent against the other parent, whatever the residential position, always assuming that the proposed course of action is consistent with the child's welfare.[21]

The second type of case is of those children aged 16 or over but still at school. The 1993 Act applies equally to the 16-year-old so that in principle parents still have a right of withdrawal. Further, under the Children Act the court may not make a section 8 order in respect of a child over 16, other than in 'exceptional circumstances' (s.9(7)). It is important to reflect on the reasoning behind these restrictions. It is that the 16-year-old enjoys a high level of legal independence while still technically a minor. Thus, a young person of this age is free to leave school, is not subject to employment restrictions, is free to consent to medical treatment and operations, free to marry with parental consent and, in the case of girls (and most significantly for present purposes) free to engage in sexual intercourse.[22] Scots law has largely emancipated the 16-year-old from restrictions on civil capacity (Age of Legal Capacity (Scotland) Act 1991). And the courts have long recognised the futility of ordering young people of this age to subject themselves to parental control (*Krishnan v Sutton L.B.C.* [1970] Ch. 181). The Education Act 1993 is, frankly, downright inconsistent with the general level of legal autonomy enjoyed by the 16-year-old. It is entirely likely that a court would, first, find that the circumstances were exceptional and, secondly, intervene to give effect to the wishes of a 16-year-old to receive sex education. The only qualification is perhaps that a different view might be taken of the child of this age with learning difficulties. But in this case it might be contended that it is precisely this more vulnerable child who might be most in need of the protection which sensitive and appropriate sex education could offer.

Advice and counselling

The Department for Education's circular entitled *Sex Education in Schools* of 6 May 1994 (5/94 superseding Circular No.11/87) purports to advise on the issue of counselling and advice given by teachers to individual pupils, especially concerning pupils' own sexual behaviour (paras. 38-42). More accurately, it hints about it, for the advice given (if such it may be termed) is so vague and ill-founded that if given by an undergraduate it would probably merit a third class! Schools are told that dealings between teachers and pupils 'should never trespass on the proper exercise of parental rights and responsibilities' (para. 38). What exactly is this supposed to mean? The Circular then moves on specifically to contraceptive advice to pupils under the age of 16. It states: 'The general rule must be that giving an individual pupil advice on such matters without parental knowledge or consent would be an inappropriate exercise of a teacher's professional responsibilities'. And there is a dark hint at illegality: 'Teachers are not health professionals, and the legal position of a teacher giving advice in such circumstances has never been tested in the courts'. This seems to me to be, at one and the same time, a rewriting of the *Gillick* decision and a thinly-veiled attempt to intimidate the teaching profession. I hope to demonstrate that it is without foundation in criminal or civil law.

Taking the criminal law first, the suggestion is that a teacher advising on contraception or related matters could be a secondary party to the offence of unlawful sexual intercourse under section 6 of the Sexual Offences Act 1956 (para. 39). It has also been suggested that there could be criminal responsibility under section 28(1) of that Act, which makes it an offence 'to cause or encourage the prostitution of, or the commission of unlawful sexual intercourse with, or of an indecent assault on, a girl under the age of 16 for whom he is responsible'. We can quickly dispose of the latter offence on the basis that a teacher is not within the statutory definition of 'responsible' persons.[23] So far as section 6 is concerned, the majority of the House of Lords in *Gillick* were clearly of the view that a *doctor* who gave advice on contraception would not aid or abet that offence provided that he acted in good faith, as a matter of professional responsibility, to protect the young woman against the potential adverse effects of sexually transmitted disease or unwanted pregnancy. By analogy, the teacher who responds to a pupil's request for advice will not commit an offence provided that he or she also acts in a professional manner and with genuine motives.[24] The position would of course be different if the teacher actively encouraged under-age pupils to engage in sexual intercourse but this seems so unlikely as to be scarcely worthy of comment.

Let me now take the alternative suggestion that a teacher might act unlawfully in 'trespassing on the proper exercise of parental responsibilities'. To sustain this argument it would be necessary to explain precisely *why* such action would be unlawful. The only conceivable possibilities are that the teacher would commit a tort against the child or against the parent. It is difficult to see how merely talking to a child could be tortious. Advice-giving can conceivably be tortious where it amounts to negligent misstatement (*Hedley Byrne & Co. v Heller & Partners* [1964] A.C. 465), but assuming that the teacher acted responsibly and professionally, referring the child to other appropriately qualified professionals, no tort could possibly arise. What about a tort against the parent? This suggestion is now quite unsustainable in the light of the unambiguous ruling of the Court of Appeal in *F v Wirral M.B.C.* ([1991] 2 WLR 1132) that there is no tort of interference with parental rights (the former action for loss of a child's services was abolished by the Administration of Justice Act 1982). The parent, by virtue of parental responsibility, has no right or claim *independent* of the child's, which can found a civil action.

It therefore seems plain that advice-giving and counselling could be neither criminal nor tortious. If the Government believes that it could be unlawful in some other way I would be interested to hear the arguments.

I take this to be the automatic position arising by operation of law. And it is difficult to see how it could be otherwise. If it were to be regarded as unlawful merely to talk to children, where would it all end? Why confine the issue to schools? Many people might be approached by children for advice on a host of matters – the relative, the trusted friend, the spiritual adviser, the voluntary or professional advice agency. Must they all take care not to 'trespass on the proper exercise of parental rights and responsibilities'? Such a requirement would be impracticable and is untenable in any society which attaches importance to children's rights. It has never been the approach of family law. Family law rather allows dealings between children and third parties (assuming they are lawful activities) unless and until someone has brought an issue before the court for its adjudication. It has long been possible for parents or others[25] to apply for orders, traditionally in wardship proceedings, restraining some specific involvement between a child and an adult. Such orders have often been used to break 'undesirable associations' (a good account of the use of wardship for these purposes is to be found in Lowe and White (1979) at pp.201-205) or to determine specific issues. There would be nothing to prevent a parent seeking an order to prevent advice or counselling being given without his or her permission. But the key point is that such actions would *not* be unlawful unless and until restrained by court order. In the event of a restraining order being made it would of course be unlawful to act against it since this would amount to contempt of court. Whether or not an order would be made would depend as always on the court's view of the child's best interests.

Conclusion

The case for recognising access to sex education as a universal right of children is a peculiarly strong one since it lies at the conjunction of several different kinds of claims which are the basis of children's rights. Whether we see children's rights as claims to protection from harm, to self-determination or to the receipt of welfare benefits, sex education is an essential component. It would therefore seem to follow that the state should be required to have a strong justification for interfering with this right. The official justification for allowing a parental right of withdrawal is the primary importance the state attaches to the role of parents in raising children (see particularly para.7 of Circular 5/94). Yet the biological aspects of sex education are to remain part of the National Curriculum and therefore outside parents' control. The reforms are really a further attempt to prescribe and influence centrally the content and delivery of education.[26] The not-so-hidden agenda is to signify official disapproval of value-neutral education about extra-marital sexual activity and its potentially harmful consequences among the young. This is achieved by removing these matters from the National Curriculum and by oblique threats that individual advice and counselling may be unlawful and lead to legal action against teachers. All of this is evident in the Government's Circular which contains a section headed 'the moral framework for sex education' (DFE 1994, para.8). Thus, it is the DFE's view that sex education 'must not be value-free' but must be 'set within a clear framework of values' and that pupils should 'be encouraged to appreciate the value of stable family life, marriage and the responsibilities of parenthood'. We should not be surprised by any of this. This is, after all, the government which is keen to get 'back to basics' about these matters. But I have argued elsewhere (Bainham 1995) that to view the family centred on marriage as the only, or even the preferred, family form is contentious in a modern pluralistic society. In this context of sex education we need to remind ourselves that it is probably only a minority in society who are now committed to the idea of lifelong (as opposed to serial) monogamy and to the restriction of sexual activity to such unions. And if we, as adult society, are not prepared to accept the exclusivity of lifelong monogamy then we ought not to patronise and deceive children about the facts of life. We should certainly not allow conservative or conventional views of family life, whether held by the government of the day or individual parents, to impede the provision of information necessary to protect children from the harms which can result from early unprotected sexual activity.

I have sought to demonstrate that there is an over-emphasis on *parents'* rights in education generally and specifically in section 241 of the Education Act 1993. This jars seriously with developments elsewhere in family law which have been largely in the opposite direction, de-emphasising the rights of parents and promoting the comparatively new idea of legal rights for children. While the Children Act 1989 was referred to in the debates on the Education Bill, the references to it were usually vague and general. It must be doubted whether those responsible for the formulation of education policy have a good enough, or indeed any, understanding of the principles in the legislation or the internationally recognised rights of children.

More than anything it is necessary that the *independent* interests, claims, rights (whatever we wish to call them) of children are recognised in the educational context. And this is, in my view, an important test of the efficacy of the European Convention on Human Rights. The European Commission and Court have not as yet been as ready to recognise these independent rights as I would have wished. Nearly all the cases have concerned parents' rights vis à vis the state. Yet children are also persons with rights under the Convention and they will be affected by the decisions. I do not think that the Commission and Court should duck these wider questions simply because they are not strictly necessary to determine in order to reach a decision.[27] And whether we consider these issues on a domestic or international level we ought always to remind ourselves that education exists for the benefit of children and not for their parents.

Notes

1. It is of course important under international conventions such as the United Nations Convention on the Rights of the Child or the European Convention on Human Rights to establish that 'rights' as such exist.
2. Provision for separate representation of parents and children dates from the 1970s and is now made in section 41 of the Children Act 1989. The court is now required to appoint a guardian *ad litem* for the child in every case of care or supervision proceedings 'unless satisfied that it is not necessary to do so in order to safeguard his interests'.
3. See the speech of Baroness Jay of Paddington referring to the concerns of the NSPCC on this matter: H.L. Debs, 6 July 1993 col. 1295.
4. For a recent collection of academic writings on children's rights, see Alston, P, Parker, S and Seymour, J (1992) *Children, Rights and the Law*. Oxford University Press.

5. The Children Act 1989 makes provision for proper consideration of children's views in the statutory checklist of factors which the courts must consider in determining disputes over children. See also section 22(4) and (5) which require local authorities to have regard to the wishes and feelings of children when taking decisions affecting them.
6. Section 36 of the Education Act 1944, which places parents under a legal duty to ensure that their child receives appropriate education between the ages of 5 and 16. Failure to do so can lead to prosecution under sections 198 and 199 of the Education Act 1993.
7. And in relation to financial support can last beyond majority where the child is in further education or undergoing training for a trade, profession or vocation, section 29(3) Matrimonial Causes Act 1973.
8. The state of New York tried to do just this by prohibiting the distribution of contraceptives to those under 16. In the Supreme Court Stevens J. likened this to the prohibition of safety helmets in order to dramatise the State's disapproval of motor cycles! See *Carey v Population Services International* 431 U.S. 678 (1977) at 715.
9. Education (No. 2) Act 1986. Section 15(4) abolished pupil governors. For a general discussion of school government see Harris (1993), Chapter 3.
10. Section 9, Education Reform Act 1988. See Harris (1993) at 226-231.
11. Adopted by the General Assembly of the UN by acclamation on 20 November 1989. The right to education is recognised in Article 28.
12. The right to education is recognised in Article 2, First Protocol.
13. Lord Judd was wrong to suggest otherwise in the House of Lords. See H.L. Debs, 6 July 1993, col. 1317 and the response of Baroness Blatch at col. 1321.
14. It has been recognised ever since *Gillick* that this does leave open the possibility of manipulation by the person dealing with the child. There must be a risk that where the adult disagrees with the child he will simply deem the child to be incompetent.
15. Hence it does not apply in the medical context to the child aged *over* 16 since the child of this age is declared by section 8(1) Family Law Reform Act 1969 to be competent to consent to any surgical, medical or dental treatment.

16. This aspect of the *Gillick* decision is frequently overlooked by some child liberationists who appear to think that all decision-making involving adolescents is, or ought to be, governed by the maturity test.
17. *Re SC (A Minor) (Leave to Seek Residence Order)* [1994] 1 FLR 96. For a commentary on both decisions see Bainham (1994).
18. The principle in section 1(1) of the Children Act 1989 that when a court is determining any question regarding the upbringing of a child 'the child's welfare shall be the court's paramount consideration'.
19. I am using this expression to include both 'non-residential' parents where a residence order has been made and the numerically far more significant category of parents who are not primary caretakers where no order has been made.
20. Under the old law the courts would occasionally make so-called 'split' orders giving custody to the parent without care and control. See *Jane v Jane* (1983) FLR 712.
21. For an example in the educational context see *Re P (A Minor) (Education)* [1992] 1 FLR 316 where the wishes of a 14 year old boy to attend a day school rather than boarding school were held to be decisive where his father and mother were in dispute. See also *Re S* [1992] 2 FLR 313.
22. The girl herself commits no criminal offence if she has intercourse under the age of 16 (*R v Tyrell* [1894] 1 QB 710) but the man concerned commits the offence of unlawful sexual intercourse irrespective of her consent to the intercourse.
23. Section 28(3) as amended by the Children Act 1989 defines responsible persons to include the girl's 'parents'; 'any person who is not a parent of hers but who has general responsibility for her'; and 'any person who has care of her'.
24. It must be said that this position, while justifiable on grounds of social policy, does not sit at all well with the orthodox principles of complicity under criminal law. As a general rule motives, as distinct from intention, are irrelevant and it is possible to aid or abet an offence even though there is no desire for it to be committed. See, for example, *R v Bainbridge* [1960] 1 QB 129.
25. Wardship would often be the only available remedy under the old law because of the strict rules of locus standi applying to other proceedings involving children. Now anyone may apply for a section 8 order under the Children Act 1989 with leave of the court.

26. Apart from the creation of the National Curriculum itself, other more controversial examples are sections 7 and 8 of the Education Reform Act 1988 requiring religious education and collective worship in schools to reflect the mainly Christian religious traditions of the U.K., and section 44 of the Education (No. 2) Act 1986, which requires governing bodies to prohibit 'the pursuit of partisan political activities' in state schools.
27. Recent examples are *Hoffmann v Austria* (1993) Publ. Eur. Ct. H.R. Series A, No. 255C (1994) Camb. L.J. 39 and *Keegan v Ireland* (1994) Publ. Eur. Ct. H.R., Series A No. 290.

3. Don't tell the children: The Department's guidance on the provision of information about contraception to individual pupils

Jo Bridgeman, Lecturer in Law, The University of Liverpool

Introduction

The Department for Education Circular 5/94 on Sex Education in Schools fails to provide clear guidance to teachers as to the information which they can lawfully impart to an individual pupil who approaches them for advice about contraception. It merely indicates that the legal position is uncertain. This chapter explores the House of Lords' decision in *Gillick v West Norfolk and Wisbech Area Health Authority and another* [1986] 1 AC 112 and the application of that decision, beyond health professionals, to teachers. This chapter further considers whether a teacher who provides an individual pupil under the age of 16 with information about contraception or suggests where that pupil could obtain professional advice will be committing a criminal offence. As young people who seek advice from adults other than their own parents may be concerned that their parents are not told, a further question is whether teachers can provide such advice to pupils in confidence. It is important that young people are provided with the knowledge which will enable them to protect themselves from all the undesirable consequences of sexual activity and to develop the 'responsible attitude' towards sex that the Government states to be one of the aims of sex education.

The most recent Department for Education Circular on *Sex Education in Schools* (DFE 1994) does little to give guidance to school teachers about their legal position when approached by an individual pupil for advice on contraception. The Circular, without examining the relevant law, merely states:

> Particular care must be exercised in relation to contraceptive advice to pupils under 16, for whom sexual intercourse is unlawful. The general rule must be that giving an individual pupil advice on such matters without parental knowledge or consent would be an inappropriate exercise of a teacher's professional responsibilities. Teachers are not health professionals, and the legal position of a teacher giving advice in such circumstances has never been tested in the courts (DFE 1994, para. 39).

It is correct to state that the courts have never specifically considered the question of whether a teacher can lawfully provide information about contraception to an individual pupil. However, the guidance is misleading in that it categorically dismisses the issue without exploring how the decision of the House of Lords in *Gillick v West Norfolk and Wisbech Area Health Authority and another* [1986] 1 AC 112 can be applied beyond health professionals. The House of Lords accepted that, in some circumstances, a doctor could provide a girl under the age of 16 with contraceptive advice or treatment without committing a criminal offence.[1] Further, in these cases, that advice could be given without informing her parents or obtaining their consent. Can their Lordships' reasoning be extended to teachers? This question cannot be properly addressed in isolation from the policy considerations advanced in *Gillick*, put into their contemporary context.

In *Gillick,* judicial attention was directed to the contraceptive pill, 'unknown to our fathers but of immense consequence to society', which had, in the opinion of Lord Scarman, 'introduced a new independence, and offers new options, for women' ([1986] 1 AC 112, per Lord Scarman at 176D). Whilst the contraceptive pill has become a popular method of birth control since it was approved for use in Britain in the early sixties,[2] other methods of family limitation – abortion, infanticide, withdrawal, barrier methods and spermicide – have been employed for centuries. Birth control services were available in Britain from early in the twentieth century but it was not until 1967 that the State sanctioned the provision of contraception.[3] Section 1 of the National Health Service (Family Planning) Act 1967 empowered local health authorities to provide contraceptive services. Since 1977 the Secretary of State has been under a duty, imposed by section 5(1)(b) of the National Health Service Act 1977, to

> arrange, to such extent as he considers necessary to meet all reasonable requirements in England and Wales, for the giving of advice on

> contraception, the medical examination of persons seeking advice on contraception, the treatment of such persons and the supply of contraceptive substances and appliances.

The legislation imposing this duty makes no reference to the age of the person to whom contraceptive services must be made available. Whilst adolescence may be a time for exploration of sexual feelings and experimentation in sexual behaviour, sexual activity amongst young people is frequently portrayed as inappropriate conduct which should be prohibited or prevented. Reflecting this, the provision of contraceptives and contraceptive advice to young people remains controversial.

The Provision of Contraceptive Advice

Section 1 of the Education Reform Act 1988 states that the school curriculum must be 'balanced and broadly based' and should promote 'the spiritual, moral, cultural, mental and physical development of pupils at the school and of society' and prepare 'such pupils for the opportunities, responsibilities and experiences of adult life'. It is explained in the DFE Circular that in order to fulfil this requirement schools should include in the curriculum a 'comprehensive, well-planned programme of sex education' (DFE 1994, para. 3). Section 241 of the Education Act 1993, which came into force on 1 September 1994, imposed upon all maintained secondary schools the legal duty to provide sex education. As before, sex education must foster in pupils a regard for 'moral considerations and the value of family life' (s.46 Education (No. 2) Act 1986). The legislation provides that sex education includes (but, presumably, is not limited to) education about HIV, AIDS and other sexually transmitted diseases (s.241(2) of the Education Act 1993 inserting this definition into s.114(1) of the Education Act 1944). The guidance expands upon this by outlining what, in the view of the Secretary of State, should be covered in sex education classes in secondary schools. Classes should address both the facts about human reproduction and the emotional and ethical issues surrounding it. It is further stated that pupils should, at an appropriate point in their secondary school career, receive lessons about HIV, AIDS and other sexually transmitted diseases, and within the broad heading 'human reproductive processes and behaviour' it is recommended that they should also learn about contraception and abortion. Whatever aspect of sex education is being addressed, the aim of the school should always be 'to offer balanced and factual information and to acknowledge the major moral and ethical issues involved' (DFE 1994, para. 11). The purpose of sex education is, in the view of the Secretary of State, to:

> provide knowledge about loving relationships, the nature of sexuality and the processes of human reproduction. In addition, it should lead to the acquisition of understanding and attitudes which prepare pupils to view their relationships in a responsible and healthy manner. It must not be value-free; it should also be tailored not only to the age but also to the understanding of pupils. The Secretary of State believes that schools' programmes of sex education should therefore aim to present facts in an objective, balanced and sensitive manner, set within a clear framework of values and an awareness of the law on sexual behaviour. Pupils should accordingly be encouraged to appreciate the value of stable family life, marriage and the responsibilities of parenthood. They should be helped to consider the importance of self-restraint, dignity, respect for themselves and others, acceptance of responsibility, sensitivity towards the needs and views of others, loyalty and fidelity. And they should be enabled to recognise the physical, emotional and moral implications, and risks, of certain types of behaviour, and to accept that both sexes must behave responsibly in sexual matters (DFE 1994, para. 8).

The present circular maintains the distinction, drawn in the circular issued in 1987 following the House of Lords' decision in *Gillick*, between providing sex education classes and the position of teachers when approached by an individual pupil for advice, particularly when it is apparent that the pupil is seeking information related to their own sexual conduct. The guidance states that in the latter instance the 'pastoral interests of teachers in the welfare and well-being of pupils must never trespass on the proper exercise of parental rights and responsibilities' (DFE 1994, para. 38). Whilst the guidance recommends that facts about contraception should be presented as part of sex education, teachers are warned that if they provide individual pupils with advice about contraception their legal position is not entirely clear. How are teachers to explain this distinction to pupils? Some pupils will find sex education classes extremely embarrassing and may not feel able to ask any questions which they have during the course of the lesson. If an alternative opportunity for asking such questions is not available the pupil may be left in ignorance. Further, as Lesley Holly emphasises, the plain facts about contraception only go so far. To be of any real use, the pupil must be able to understand how those facts apply to them (Holly, 1989, p.75). Christine Farrell and Leonie Kellaher suggest that there are two types of sex education. In the first the teacher provides the pupil with a knowledge base of information about the relevant facts and moral and ethical considerations. The second involves teaching pupils how this knowledge is relevant to them so that they can use it to deal with their own sexual feelings, desires and needs (Farrell and Kellaher, 1978, p.139). Only if both of these are provided will pupils be in a position to be responsible in their sexual behaviour. To fulfil both, the teacher must be able to answer questions about contraception from individual pupils, even on matters relating to their own sexual experiences.

The distinction which the guidance makes has to be explored in the context of two questions raised by the provision of contraceptive advice to individual pupils relating to their own sexual needs: the legality of the provision of advice; and, whether the pupil can be assured that they can seek, and be provided with, advice in confidence.

Legality

In December 1980, the DHSS issued guidance to area health authorities on family planning services for young people. This was a revised version of parts of an earlier Memorandum of Guidance on Family Planning Services. The guidance noted the sensitive nature of the problems raised when a young person under the age of 16 sought contraceptive advice and treatment. Whilst it was emphasised that doctors should attempt to persuade the young person to involve their parents, it did acknowledge that there were 'exceptional' circumstances when confidential advice and treatment could be provided. A mother of five daughters under the age of 16, Mrs Gillick, objected to the guidance and sought assurance from her area health authority that none of her daughters would be provided with contraceptive or abortion services without her knowledge. When this assurance was not forthcoming she instituted proceedings against the DHSS and the area health authority, seeking a declaration that the advice given in the guidance was unlawful and a further declaration against the area health authority that none of their employees could provide her daughters with contraceptive or abortion services without her knowledge and consent. The case, *Gillick v West Norfolk and Wisbech Area Health Authority and another* [1986] 1 AC 112, reached the House of Lords, where their Lordships considered three issues in order to determine whether to grant the declaration sought. The question of fundamental importance to this chapter is whether a doctor who gives contraceptive advice or treatment to a young person aged under 16 without parental consent incurs criminal liability.[4] There was little agreement amongst the judiciary as the case progressed through the courts, although the issue was finally resolved by a majority decision of the House of Lords that no criminal offence would be committed.

In *Gillick*, which were the courts asked to rule on the case focused upon the problem presented by the provision of contraceptive advice and treatment to girls under the age of 16. The reasons for this focus were twofold: first, the facts which were presented to the courts raised the question of the provision of contraceptive advice and treatment to Mrs Gillick's five daughters; and secondly, because, practically speaking, in the absence of medical methods of contraception operating upon the body of the male, it will be the female who is seeking the advice of, and treatment from, a health professional. Given the criminal offences in question, this section concentrates initially upon the legality of the provision of advice to girls under the age of 16 before addressing the question of liability when advice is sought by a male.

The contention concerning criminal liability was originally advanced on two grounds. First, it was claimed before Woolf J in the High Court that the guidance provided amounted to advice to doctors to commit an offence contrary to section 28 of the Sexual Offences Act 1956. This states that:

> [i]t is an offence for a person to cause or encourage ... the commission of unlawful sexual intercourse with...a girl under the age of 16 for whom he is responsible.

Either of the girl's parents, anyone who has parental responsibility for her or anyone who has care of her is, for the purposes of this section, 'responsible' for her (s. 28(3) Sexual Offences Act 1956). Counsel argued that a girl who attends a clinic for advice and treatment is, at that time, in the care of the doctor or clinic. Woolf J considered that this interpretation stretched too far the terms of the statute and that a doctor would not be criminally liable contrary to this section. In the Court of Appeal, this section was not explored as counsel for both sides accepted that the liability of the doctor depended entirely upon the facts. Consequently, the focus in the House of Lords was on the second contention, that a doctor who provided contraceptive advice or treatment would be a secondary participant by aiding or abetting an offence contrary to the Sexual Offences Act 1956. By virtue of section 5 of that Act:

> It is [an offence] for a man to have unlawful sexual intercourse with a girl under the age of thirteen.

Section 6 provides that:

> It is an offence...for a man to have unlawful sexual intercourse with a girl...under the age of sixteen.

The girl's sexual partner would commit an offence contrary to one of these sections, depending upon her age. The offence contrary to section 5 is the more serious offence and carries a maximum penalty of life imprisonment. Section 6 carries a maximum penalty of five years imprisonment. Subsections 2 and 3 provide two specific defences; first, that the man reasonably believed that he was legally married to the girl, and secondly, 'the young man's defence'. This provides a defence to a man under the age of 24 who had reasonable cause to believe that the girl was 16 or older and who had not previously been charged with a similar offence (s. 6(2) and (3) Sexual Offences Act 1956).

Would the doctor be an accomplice to the commission of the offence? The *actus reus* of accomplice liability is to aid, abet, counsel or procure the commission of any offence.[5] These terms are given their 'ordinary meaning' (*Attorney General's Reference (No. 1 of 1975)* [1975] QB 773, at 779E). In modern terms 'aid' can be understood to mean to help, support or assist and 'abet' to encourage. The House of Lords accepted that giving contraceptive advice and treatment to an under age girl encouraged or assisted unlawful sexual intercourse. In their Lordships' opinion the risk of an unwanted pregnancy deters young people from engaging in sexual activity. Lord Brandon, for example, suggested that the decision to consult a doctor indicates that the girl is aware of the risk of an unwanted pregnancy:

> [T]o give such a girl advice about contraception, to examine her with a view to her using one or more forms of protection, and finally to prescribe contraceptive treatment for her, necessarily involves promoting, encouraging, or facilitating the having of sexual intercourse, contrary to public policy, by that girl with a man ([1986] 1 AC 112, at 197B).

A professional who provides contraceptive advice and treatment to an under-age girl may have committed the *actus reus* of the offence and will have done so if she then has sexual intercourse. As the act of the aider or abettor does not need to be the cause of the criminal offence, it is irrelevant that unlawful sexual intercourse would have taken place anyway.

However, to establish criminal liability it is also necessary to prove that the professional had the necessary *mens rea* when committing the *actus reus* of the offence. The debate surrounding participatory liability in which *Gillick* partakes is whether the *mens rea* is merely an intention to do acts which the professional knew to be capable of assisting or encouraging the commission of the crime, or whether the accomplice must also have intended that the crime be committed. If all that is required is that the professional intentionally did an act which he or she knew to be capable of assisting or encouraging the commission of the crime, the *mens rea* is satisfied when the professional provides contraceptive advice or treatment. The argument that he or she did not intend for the offence contrary to the Sexual Offences Act 1956 to be committed would be irrelevant to criminal liability. In *NCB v Gamble* [1959] 1 QB 11, for example, it was held that the defendant did not need to intend for the crime to be committed. The defendant was liable for aiding and abetting even though he was indifferent as to whether the crime was committed or not; all that was required for accomplice liability was that the defendant intentionally did an act knowing of the circumstances which made it capable of assisting or encouraging the commission of a crime. In comparison, in *Fretwell* (1862) Le & Ca 161, the defendant had obtained poison for use as an abortifacient at the insistence of the deceased who threatened to kill herself if he did not do so. He was acquitted of being an accessory to murder when she died as a result of taking the abortifacient because he had thought, and hoped, that she would change her mind about using it. The defendant was not indifferent as to whether the crime was committed, he hoped that it would not be committed.

In *Gillick*, the majority (Lords Fraser, Bridge and Scarman) emphasised that criminal liability would depend upon the intention of the doctor. Whilst a doctor who gave a girl contraceptive advice or treatment with the intention of facilitating unlawful sexual intercourse may well be guilty of a criminal offence, Lords Scarman and Bridge said that a doctor who gave contraceptive advice or treatment to a girl under 16, honestly intending to act in the girl's best interests, would not be criminally liable. In their Lordships' opinion, this meant that the doctor could prescribe contraception to a girl under the age of 16 only if she had the capacity to consent or, following the DHSS guidance, in 'exceptional circumstances'. Lord Scarman continued:

> The adjective 'clinical' emphasises that it must be a medical judgement based upon what he honestly believes to be necessary for the physical, mental, and emotional health of his patient. The bona fide exercise by a doctor of his clinical judgement must be a complete negation of the guilty mind which is an essential ingredient of the criminal offence of aiding and abetting the commission of unlawful sexual intercourse ([1986] 1 AC 112, at 190G).

Lord Scarman emphasised that '[i]f the prescription is the bona fide exercise of his clinical judgement as to what is best for his patient's health, he has nothing to fear from the criminal law or from any public policy based on the criminality of a man having sexual intercourse with her' ([1986] 1 AC 112, at 191A).

The majority held that it was necessary to establish that the accomplice intended that the crime be committed. However, to avoid liability on the part of the doctor they gave the concept of intention a narrower interpretation than it is usually given in criminal law. A person acts with intention when it is his or her purpose or aim to bring something about. Further, the jury may infer that the defendant acted intentionally where the defendant foresaw that consequence which was virtually certain to result from his or her voluntary act (*R v Moloney* [1985] AC 905). Thus, it must surely be arguable that a doctor who gives contraceptive advice or treatment intends a crime contrary to the Sexual Offences Act 1956 to be committed if the doctor foresees unlawful sexual intercourse to be the virtually certain consequence of the provision of advice or treatment. The majority considered intention only in the sense of the doctor's purpose which, in their Lordships' opinion, was not to facilitate the crime of unlawful sexual intercourse but to avoid the consequences of an unwanted pregnancy. It must be acknowledged that there has been much criticism of the approach taken by the majority and preference expressed for the views of the conflicting authorities which suggest that all that is required is that the accessory intends to do an act which he or she knows to be capable of facilitating the commission of a crime and that it is irrelevant whether the accessory intends for the crime to be committed or not.[6] The decision of the majority can be criticised for a distortion of the accepted meaning of intention in criminal law employed to reach the conclusion that the doctor would commit no criminal offence. At the same time, however, this is the fundamental significance of the decision in *Gillick*. Presumably, the judiciary perceived the provision of contraceptive advice and treatment to young persons by health professionals to be socially desirable. In the absence of any available defence, the distortion of the accepted legal meaning of intention was necessary to facilitate the provision of contraception to young people (Ashworth, 1991, p. 153).

In the guidance issued by the Department of Education and Science following *Gillick*, teachers were advised that as far as providing contraceptive advice to an individual pupil under 16 was concerned, 'the general rule must be that giving an individual pupil advice on such matters without parental knowledge or consent would be an inappropriate exercise of a teacher's professional responsibilities, and could, depending on the circumstances, amount to a criminal offence' (DES 1987, para. 26). The guidance referred to the recent (as it was then) House of Lords decision in *Gillick*:

> The House of Lords found that, while it should be most unusual for a doctor to provide such a service to a child under 16 without parental knowledge or consent, there were circumstances, described in the judgements, where he or she would be justified in doing so. These circumstances hinged essentially upon the nature and context of medical advice and treatment in connection with the supply and use of contraceptive devices. They have no parallel in school education.

Thus, from the outset, the Department of Education and Science was not prepared to address the extent to which the reasoning of the House of Lords in *Gillick* applied beyond health professionals. In April 1993, the Department for Education proposed a revision of the guidelines (which was not implemented) but maintained the view that a teacher who provided contraceptive advice to an individual pupil could commit a criminal offence (DFE 1993a, para. 30). In *The Independent on Sunday* (24 April 1993) it was reported that, in an attempt to justify his refusal to alter this guidance, John Patten ordered education officials to find out what evidence there was on the effects of sex education on the sexual behaviour of young people. A spokesperson for the Department for Education was quoted in *The Independent* (2 May 1993): 'Our understanding is that teachers who give advice on contraception for under-16s are breaking the law. The law is the law. For us to change the guidelines, the law would have to change.' Not surprisingly, therefore, there was no change to the Department for Education Draft Circular on sex education in schools, following the Education Act 1993, in December 1993 (DFE 1993b). The latest guidance does not warn teachers that they may incur criminal liability for abetting unlawful intercourse, but rather expresses uncertainty as to the exact legal position of teachers: 'Teachers are not health professionals, and the legal position of a teacher giving advice in such circumstances has not been tested in the courts' (DFE 1994, para. 39).

Is the decision in *Gillick* limited to health professionals, so that a teacher who provided contraceptive advice to a pupil under the age of 16 would commit a criminal offence? Lord Fraser stated that as the case was concerned with guidance contained in a DHSS circular, 'the appeal therefore only directly concerns doctors and other persons working in the NHS' ([1986] 1 AC 112, at 165H). However, it is possible, without usurping the function of the courts, to consider the legal principles relied upon and the policy arguments accepted, to speculate upon their applicability to other professionals such as school teachers. The guidelines issued by John Patten reveal his own (and the Government's) moral stance, providing a conservative interpretation of the decision. It is further contrary to the spirit of *Gillick* which 'supports rather than detracts from the legal entitlement of mature adolescents to approach professionals for advice' (Bainham, 1988, p. 186).

Can the reasoning employed to deny that a health professional would be criminally liable be applied to the school teacher who gives advice to a pupil, or is that relationship significantly different? Whether a teacher who gave an individual pupil information about contraception would commit the *actus reus* by encouraging or assisting unlawful sexual intercourse cannot be determined without considering the kind of advice a teacher would be able to give. Whilst a doctor may prescribe the contraceptive pill, fit an IUD or diaphragm, or provide the injectable or implantable contraceptives, a teacher will only be in a position either to explain what options are available and inform the pupil which of these methods can be purchased 'over the counter', or to suggest that the pupil seeks further professional advice. However, the court may still feel that a teacher who gave such advice would be helping or encouraging unlawful sexual intercourse. Liability would, therefore, as with health professionals, turn upon the state of mind of the teacher.

In *Gillick* the House of Lords, focusing upon the clinical judgement of a doctor, held that no criminal liability would follow if the doctor acted in what he or she honestly believed to be in the girl's best interests, and not with the intention that a crime contrary to the Sexual Offences Act 1956 be committed. Any court addressing the legal position of teachers would consider the judgments of the majority in *Gillick* and could apply their Lordships' reasoning (Levy 1994). There would be evidence from which the jury could conclude that the purpose of a teacher who gave a pupil contraceptive advice, having made the professional judgement that it was in the pupil's best interests, would be to avoid an unwanted pregnancy not to facilitate unlawful sexual intercourse. Therefore, the Department for Education guidelines would have been more useful if they had explained the reasons given by the judiciary in *Gillick* for reaching the conclusion that they did on the criminal law issue. They could have then continued to emphasise the need for teachers to exercise their professional judgement to act in the best interests of the individual pupil in each case and suggested the kind of factors which may be of relevance when deciding the content of the vague notion of 'best interests'.

Lord Brandon, giving a dissenting judgment, considered that the doctor who provided contraceptive advice and treatment to a girl under the age of 16 would commit a criminal offence. In his Lordship's opinion, as it was an unlawful act for a man to have sexual intercourse with a girl under the age of 16, it necessarily amounted to a criminal offence for any person to promote, encourage or facilitate such an act. If the letter of the law is applied, anyone – doctor, parent, brother, sister, friend, youth worker – who provides contraceptive advice to a young person would aid and abet the offence contrary to section 5 or 6 of the Sexual Offences Act 1956. It is not possible to distinguish between doctors, teachers (or other professionals) and other adults, including the child's own parents. Teachers could not, as the guidance implies, be trespassing upon parental rights by providing pupils with such information, as parents would have no right to give their children such information but would incur criminal liability if they did so. This interpretation of the law seems to add weight to the contrary conclusion that, in certain circumstances, teachers can lawfully provide information to pupils under the age of 16. To determine otherwise would deny young people under the age of 16 *any* information about contraception of relevance to their own sexual needs.

The next issue to be explored is the legal position of the teacher who is approached by a male pupil for advice on contraception. The law has long sought to protect 'under-age' girls from heterosexual intercourse by imposing criminal liability for unlawful sexual intercourse with girls under the age of consent. There are no comparable offences to protect young boys. However, it is an offence contrary to section 15 of the 1956 Act 'for a person to make an indecent assault on a man'. Whilst consent negatives this offence, a person under the age of 16 cannot give a valid consent (s. 15(2) Sexual Offences Act 1956). If a boy seeks advice about contraception because he participates in consensual sexual intercourse with a woman over the age of 16, he likewise becomes the victim the law seeks to protect, his consent being legally invalid. In such circumstances the question arises whether the teacher may be aiding or abetting the commission of a crime upon the male pupil. Alternatively, it may be a question whether the teacher would be aiding and abetting the male pupil to commit a crime contrary to sections 5 or 6 of the Sexual Offences Act 1956 if the teacher knows that the pupil's sexual partner is a girl under the age of 16.[7] The same reasoning applies to the provision of advice to male pupils as to female pupils, as long as the intention of the teacher was not to encourage unlawful sexual intercourse but to avoid the unwanted consequences of sexual activity. It is hoped that sex education will encourage pupils 'to accept that both sexes must behave responsibly in sexual matters' (DFE Circular 5/94, 1994, para. 8). To argue that the purpose of providing contraceptive advice to male pupils is to facilitate unlawful sexual intercourse and not to avoid an unwanted pregnancy perpetuates the notion of lack of male responsibility. To foster such a perception would be a retrograde step. To support the contrary view could encourage young people to talk to each other about the method of contraception they will use. This will be particularly important where relying upon one of the less invasive forms of contraception, such as condoms, which depend for their effective use upon the co-operation of the male partner.

The criticism by the Sex Education Forum in their response to Circular 5/94 is apt: 'As it stands the advice is confusing, offers little support or reassurance to teachers and little acknowledgement of the needs of young people...' (Sex Education Forum 1994). Stating simply that the guidance can give teachers no advice because the legal position of teachers has not been tested in the courts seeks to use uncertainty to effect the particular moral stance which those devising the guidelines wished to reflect. The Circular is only issued as guidance and, as emphasised, does not provide an authoritative statement of the law (DFE Circular 5/94, 1994, para. 1). The guidance does, however, interpret the law in a way which fails to reflect the approach taken to the issue in *Gillick*. Teachers are not health professionals and there is no judicial determination of the issue as far as teachers are concerned. But the advice could be given that, following the approach of the House of Lords in *Gillick*, teachers who give information about contraception or suggest to pupils where professional advice can be obtained, in a bona fide exercise of their professional judgement and honestly intending to act in the pupil's best interests, would have little to fear by way of criminal liability; because, as with health professionals, they would lack the intention that a crime contrary to the Sexual Offences Act 1956 be committed.

Confidentiality

The legal duty of confidentiality arises either from an express or implied term in a contract or in equity (*AG v Guardian Newspa-*

pers Ltd (No 2) [1988] 3 All ER 545, per Lord Keith at 639F). Originating in a duty imposed upon employees to respect the commercial secrets of their employer, it is now applied, in the absence of privacy laws, to protect personal information confidential to the individual. The scope of the legal duty of confidentiality is uncertain, and thus the question whether such a duty exists between teacher and pupil is necessarily speculative. In *Gillick v West Norfolk and Wisbech Area Health Authority and another* (above), the House of Lords did not specifically address the issue of confidentiality. However, the implication within the majority judgments is that a doctor does owe a duty of confidentiality to a patient under the age of 16 if she has the capacity to consent or if 'exceptional circumstances' exist, as in both situations the doctor can provide contraceptive advice or treatment without the knowledge or consent of her parents.

The 1987 Circular on Sex Education advised teachers that if approached by an individual pupil for advice about contraception the teacher should try and persuade the pupil to seek this advice from his or her parents. Further, the guidance stated that teachers were under a general duty to advise pupils of the risks of their behaviour if it put them 'in moral or physical danger, or in breach of the law'. Whether the teacher should then inform the head was for the teacher to decide according to their professional judgement. If the head was informed, it was for him or her to decide whether to involve parents, specialist support services or the local education authority (DES Circular 11/87, 1987, para. 27). The draft guidelines of December 1993 removed much of the discretion from teachers, stating that if the teacher is led to 'believe that the pupil has embarked upon, or is contemplating, a course of conduct which is likely to place him or her at moral or physical risk or in breach of the law' the teacher should *normally* inform the head teacher, who should, 'where the pupil is under age, *ensure* that the parents are made aware' (DFE, 1993b, para. 39, emphasis added). Likewise, the present guidance does not give teachers the assurance they will require if they are to feel able to give pupils advice in confidence:

> Accordingly a teacher approached by an individual pupil for specific advice on contraception or other aspects of sexual behaviour should, wherever possible, encourage the pupil to seek advice from his or her parents, and, if appropriate, from the relevant health service professional (e.g. the pupil's GP or the school doctor or nurse). Where the circumstances are such as to lead the teacher to believe that the pupil has embarked upon, or is contemplating, a course of conduct which is

> likely to place him or her at moral or physical risk or in breach of the law, the teacher has a general responsibility to ensure that the pupil is aware of the implications and is urged to seek advice as above. In such circumstances, the teacher should arrange for the pupil to be counselled if appropriate and, where the pupil is under age, for the parents to be made aware, preferably by the pupil himself or herself (and in that case checking that it has been done). Whether the specialist support services (including school health professionals) or the local education authority should also be involved will depend upon the particular circumstances involved and the professional judgement of the staff (DFE, 1994, para. 40).

A pupil who seeks the advice of their teacher will probably want to be assured of the confidentiality of the consultation. However, there are three requirements which must be fulfilled before a legal duty of confidentiality will exist (*AG v Guardian Newspapers Ltd (No 2)* [1988] 3 All ER 545, per Lord Griffiths at 649A):

i. *The information must have the necessary quality of confidence about it.* What this is referring to is clearer in the context of commerce, where the duty of confidentiality originates. In such a situation, information which the employee learns in the course of employment relating to their employer's trade and commercial secrets has the necessary quality of confidentiality. A further example is information given to a doctor. Whatever the doctor learns in the course of a consultation is confidential, be it that the patient has a rare and serious condition, is pregnant and requesting an abortion or is suffering from stress following a series of unfortunate and unhappy events. Not all information provided by a pupil to a teacher will have the necessary quality of confidentiality. It may be that the information is disclosed in the course of a normal conversation and because of its nature is not confidential; this may include the career aspirations of the pupil or what the pupil did over the weekend. Whether information has the necessary quality of confidence depends upon the nature of the information provided. Information about the sexual experiences of an individual would have the necessary quality of confidentiality.

ii. *The information must have been imparted in circumstances importing an obligation of confidence.* Such an obligation can arise out of particular relationships, such as the relationships of 'doctor and patient, priest and penitent, solicitor and client, banker and customer' (*AG v Guardian Newspapers Ltd (No 2)* [1988] 3 All ER 545, per Lord Keith at 639F). The question is whether the relationship of teacher and pupil is of a different nature to those outlined above or one which likewise imports an obligation of confidence.

iii. *There must be an unauthorised use of that information to the detriment of the person who communicated it.* What amounts to detriment is unclear. In the House of Lords in *AG v Guardian Newspapers Ltd (No 2)* [1988] 3 All ER 545 three different approaches were taken to its meaning. Lord Keith pointed to cases where an employee disclosed information relating to their employer's business which enabled another to use that information with consequent financial loss to the employer, as those in which there was clearly a detriment. However, his Lordship thought that an action should be available even though no financial detriment was suffered, as the law was seeking to encourage the respect of confidences. Lord Keith considered that there was a detriment when information was disclosed to someone where the confider did not want that person to have access to that information. It was not necessary for the disclosure to lead to any tangible harm to the confider (*AG v Guardian Newspapers Ltd (No 2)* [1988] 3 All ER 545 at 639G-640B). Lord Griffiths thought that detriment, in the sense of being positively harmful, had to be established, although this was not limited to financial loss (*AG v Guardian Newspapers Ltd (No 2)* [1988] 3 All ER 545 at 650J). Lord Goff wanted to keep open the question whether the plaintiff must prove detriment, whether or not it was required in any case depending upon the circumstances (*AG v Guardian Newspapers Ltd (No 2)* [1988] 3 All ER 545 at 659C). The case law does not, therefore, make it clear whether it is necessary to prove detriment and, if it is, what amounts to detriment. However, if the court considered that it was necessary to establish detriment, there would be a strong argument that a detriment is suffered when the parents of a pupil are given information by a teacher that the pupil did not want disclosed to them.

If a court were to accept that the teacher did owe the pupil a duty of confidentiality the question becomes one of whether disclosure of the confidential information would be justified in the public interest. This involves balancing conflicting interests (*AG v Guardian Newspapers Ltd (No 2)*. [1988] 3 All ER 545 at 659G). The teacher may argue that it is in the public interest to inform parents of a female pupil that she has sought advice on contraception. This could be justified on the grounds that he or she is in the best position to persuade their daughter not to engage in an activity which involves the perpetration of a criminal offence upon her (Brazier 1992, p. 340). Equally, it could be argued that disclosing such information to parents of a male pupil would be justified as it meant informing them that he was involved in a criminal activity (as either perpetrator or victim). However, underlying the majority decision in *Gillick* is the rationale that the prevention of teenage pregnancy may be best achieved by permitting young people to seek contraceptive services. To achieve such ends, young people will need to be assured of confidentiality. So, in balancing the conflicting interests, the teacher must consider the public interest in enabling young people to avoid the undesired consequences of sexual activity (Brazier 1992, p. 340).

As the guidance states, the teacher should encourage the pupil to seek advice from his or her parents, and, if appropriate, from a health professional. If the pupil refused to do so it would be a matter of professional judgement for a teacher to assess whether disclosure would be justified – an assessment which the teacher would make in the light of all the circumstances. The 'maturity' of the pupil will be one of the relevant factors which the teacher, exercising their professional judgement, will take into consideration, as will questions concerning whether the 'course of conduct… is likely to place [the pupil] at moral or physical risk or in breach of the law' (DFE 1994, para.40). This is expressed in vague terms which may be clarified by some examples. At one extreme may be the 13-year-old who, in the course of seeking the advice of her teacher on contraception, revealed that she was involved in a coercive relationship with an older man. In this case the teacher could claim that he or she was justified in informing the parents on the basis that it was in the best interests of the girl to do so. A different conclusion might arise if the pupil is nearly 16 and in a stable relationship with a person of similar age. Between these two extremes are many different possible situations and it may be more difficult for the teacher to decide on an appropriate course of action.

A teacher who makes the professional judgement that the parents of a young person should be told that their child has sought contraceptive advice and is having unlawful sexual intercourse is unlikely to be found guilty of a breach of confidence by the court. However, it should be emphasised that the teacher would have a power not a duty to inform the parent. In other words, in such circumstances the teacher may decide that it is in the best interests of the child for this information to be imparted to his or her parents, and would not be acting in breach of confidence by doing so: but if the teacher decided to respect the confidence of the pupil, the parent would have no legal action against the teacher for failing to inform them that their son or daughter had sought advice about contraception. Any claim would have to be based in the common law of negligence, which requires a duty of care and a breach of that duty which causes harm to the claimant. It is beyond the scope of this chapter to consider this issue at length. However, there is no authority which establishes that a teacher owes a duty to inform a parent of matters which a pupil imparts to them in confidence (Beloff and Mountfield 1994, para. 13.1 (ix)). In the absence of a duty to inform the parents, failure to do so cannot amount to breach. Further, an action in negligence turns upon the harm caused by the breach of duty. Even if the courts did consider that a duty was owed by the teacher to the parents, it is difficult to conceive of the harm which could be considered to have been caused by the failure of the teacher to inform the parent of the information which the pupil had confided in them, in the sense that, but for the teacher's failure to inform the parent, the harm which was caused would not have occurred.

The legal duty of confidentiality provides a vague assurance to young people that private, personal information which they tell their teachers will not be disclosed to their parents. The young people interviewed in the study carried out by Isobel Allen repeatedly expressed the fear that, if they attended a family planning clinic or their GP for contraceptive services, their parents would find out either because they would be seen there by someone who knew them or because their need for confidentiality would not be respected (Allen, 1991). In practical terms, teachers should exercise their professional judgement and in appropriate cases maintain the confidences of their pupils.

Going beyond the limits of the law

Underlying the advice in the guidance provided in the circular on the provision of information about contraception to individual pupils are the same policy factors which were adverted to in the House of Lords decision in *Gillick* and which address the wider context of the debate.

Morality

In *Gillick v West Norfolk and Wisbech Area Health Authority and another* (above), Lord Templeman considered the contention of Mrs Gillick that to provide contraceptive services to a girl under 16 would encourage her to engage in unlawful sexual activity which, in her view, 'offends basic principles of morality and religion and which ought not to be sabotaged in stealth by kind permission of the National Health Service' ([1986] 1 AC 112, at 202D). This stance conceives of one moral standpoint, one religious code, and denies the reality of the diverse society in which we now live. The relationship between law and morality is by no means unexplored territory and the judiciary do not shrink from imposing their moral standards upon the behaviour of individuals. Lord Templeman continued:

> The interests of a girl under 16 require her to be protected against sexual intercourse. Such a girl is not sufficiently mature to be allowed to decide to flout the accepted rules of society. The pornographic press and the lascivious film may falsely pretend that sexual intercourse is a form of entertainment available to females on request and to males on demand but the regular, frequent or casual practice of sexual intercourse by a girl or boy under the age of 16 cannot be beneficial to anybody and may cause harm to character and personality ([1986] 1 AC 112, at 202E-F).

Implicit within this is the view of teenage sex as exploitative, dangerous and irresponsible. This perception is formed somewhere other than in reality, as studies of sexual experiences and attitudes of teenagers reveal. In their study of young people aged between 16 and 18 Christine Farrell and Leonie Kellaher asked the question, 'Do you have any views on sex before marriage?' Half responded that they did approve of sex before marriage, and the majority of those who indicated that they had mixed feelings tended towards approval. Many of those who went on to provide additional comments explained that 'premarital sex was acceptable if it happened as a result of a stable relationship and care was taken to avoid an unwanted pregnancy' (Farrell and Kellaher, 1978, p. 20). In Anne Miller's 1994 study, 79 per cent of those asked expected to have sex before marriage, and 69 per cent agreed that they would only have sex with someone they loved (Miller 1994).

The DFE's guidance (in Circular 5/94) makes clear the moral framework within which sex education is to be situated. As the Sex Education Forum states in its response to the guidance, there is a distinction between exploring moral and ethical issues and prescribing moral values (Sex Education Forum 1994). To deny an individual pupil specific advice about contraception involves the imposition of moral values and may undermine her or his own confidence in making informed and responsible decisions.

The purpose of the criminal offences

Whilst the girl who has (hetero)sexual intercourse when under the age of 16 commits no criminal offence, even if she aids, abets or incites the intercourse, her sexual partner commits a serious criminal offence. According to the decision in *R v Tyrell* [1894] 1 QB 710 (considering earlier provisions in like terms) this is because the provisions were enacted by Parliament for the protection of young girls. The imposition of criminal liability upon a male who has sexual intercourse with a girl under the age of 16 may mean that the couple decide not to engage in sexual intercourse until she has reached the age of consent. However, as Lord Bridge acknowledged in *Gillick*, if the protection of young girls from the undesired consequences of unlawful sexual intercourse is the primary consideration it would be inconsistent to deny her contraception and put her at risk of an unwanted pregnancy if the couple still intended to engage in sexual intercourse ([1986] 1 AC 112, at 194F).

Reducing teenage pregnancy

In *Gillick v West Norfolk and Wisbech Area Health Authority and another* (*op. cit.*) Lord Templeman referred to differing opinions as to whether making contraceptive advice and treatment available to young persons would lead to an increase or decrease in pregnancies amongst girls under the age of 16. On the one hand he referred to the possibility that the availability of confidential contraceptive treatment may increase sexual activity and the demand for such treatment. He suggested that the available methods of contraception require either daily discipline (as with the oral contraceptive pill) or assertion at the time of intercourse (such as the cap, diaphragm or condom). In the absence of self-discipline or self-assertiveness the teenage pregnancy rate could be increased, not decreased, by making contraceptive services available to young people. The alternative argument was that a young person who was sexually active and denied confidential contraceptive services was at risk of an unwanted pregnancy. In his Lordship's view neither assertion was 'supported by evidence' or 'susceptible to proof' ([1986] 1 AC 112, at 203A).

The debate encapsulated by the two views outlined by Lord Templeman has an underlying premise that teenage heterosexual intercourse is 'inappropriate behaviour'. One response is to attempt to curb it; the other is that it cannot be stopped and so the undesirable consequences should be limited through sex education, contraceptive services and information which will enable young people to protect themselves against sexually transmitted diseases (Petchesky 1986, p. 210). As the Sex Education Forum stresses, teenage heterosexual activity (whether viewed by adults as improper behaviour or not) cannot be ignored (Sex Education Forum 1994). The survey *Sexual Behaviour in Britain* found that 18.7 per cent of women and 27.6 per cent of men aged 16-19 had been sexually active before the age of 16.[8] In July 1992 the Government published its Health Strategy in the White Paper, *The Health of the Nation*, with one of its stated targets being to reduce the rate of conceptions amongst the under 16s by at least 50 per cent, to 4.8 per 1,000 13-15-year-olds, by the year 2000 (Secretary of State for Health 1992, p.19). This will not be achieved through ignorance.

Conclusion

Underlying the guidance regarding the provision of information about contraception to individual pupils is the paramountcy of parental rights and responsibilities over the state's obligations to the young person and their rights. Encouraging parents to discuss matters relating to sexual behaviour with their child may be welcomed as engendering a discourse on issues which are, if not taboo, difficult to broach. However, the emphasis in the guidance upon parents as the appropriate source of this information or advice has the effect of denying young people the opportunity of seeking out alternative sources of information and advice where they are, for whatever reason, not obtainable at home. This approach raises the question of whether parents do provide their children with information about contraception and whether they would feel that their parental rights and responsibilities had been trespassed upon if their child approached and was provided with that information by a professional. Even where there is a good relationship between parent and child, issues such as sex education or, more specifically, contraception, may not be easy for either to raise for discussion. Isobel Allen's study, *Education in Sex and Personal Relationships*, reveals the difficulty that the parents and their teenagers had communicating, especially upon matters relating to sexual activity. The study revealed that 74 per cent of the 14-to-16-year-olds interviewed had never spoken to their mothers about contraception and 90% had never spoken to their fathers (Allen 1987, p.84, Table 24). The author noted that many parents, even where there was a close and trusting relationship, did not feel comfortable talking to their children about sex and contraception. The parents explained these difficulties as being due to their embarrassment and, being aware of the inadequacy of their own sex education, the fear that they did not know enough themselves or may not be able to convey what they did know to the teenagers. The author rightly noted the implications which this finding has for relying upon parents to discuss these issues with their children:

> The ecology of a parent-child relationship is very subtle and complicated, and there was evidence that both parents and their teenage children felt that discussion of some topics was too disturbing to be attempted. Relationships between parents and teenagers can be stormy enough without introducing even more potential points of embarrassment or disagreement, and it was quite clear from the study that both parents and teenagers in many cases preferred to avoid the issue (Allen, 1987, p. 90).

It may be that other adults are better placed than parents to provide young people with information and advice about contraception. Parents, whilst being the central figures in ensuring the welfare of their children, can and will work with professionals to fulfil their parental responsibility. There is no reason why the provision of information and advice about contraception should be detrimental to the parent-child relationship. However, as Rosalind Petchesky emphasises, it is vital that young people are provided with this information if they are to be in a position to use contraception effectively:

> It is not only misinformation that results in contraceptive failure but also the intricate social processes through which bits of information about reproductive biology and birth control techniques are perceived and either absorbed or shelved away. It comes closer to the truth to say that 'although sex is a social act, contraception is rarely thought of as a set of social skills. Thus, teenagers learn about the pill or the condom but they do not learn how to apply this knowledge in social situations' or how to connect the technique with the experience (real or fantasised) that the social situation conjures up. The question for feminists is not simply whether physicians or clinic personnel 'manage' women's reproductive lives poorly or adequately; rather, it is whether or under what conditions 'management' by professionals allows young women, and men, to know what they need to know to make their way through the thicket of sex and reproduction (Petchesky 1986, p.194, with reference omitted).

In the 1990s, the presence of AIDS has brought a sense of danger to sexual activity and one consequence has been the dissemination of information about safe sex practices. Knowledge is vital; without it you might, as the slogan goes, 'die of ignorance' (Gold, *THES*, 16th December 1994). The safest sex may be no sex, but it is foolish to believe that denying young people information about sex will prevent them from engaging in sexual activity. Only by being provided with adequate relevant information can young people have some control over their lives. The provision of knowledge is a means to empowerment: teenagers can be taught that they do not need to respond to peer pressure, or pressure from their partner;

they can be taught how to use methods of contraception to protect themselves from an undesired pregnancy and how to exercise an informed choice as to which of the available methods best meets their needs. Research shows that sex education does not encourage or increase sexual activity among young people but may have the opposite effect and also increase the use of safe sex practices amongst those who are already sexually active (Kirby 1995). To refuse to discuss their problems, questions or queries merely confirms the taboo nature of sexual activity. It further means that young people will be denied an opportunity to explore how the information which they receive in sex education classes applies to them.[9]

The debate concerning whether teachers can lawfully provide advice about contraception to individual pupils under the age of 16 is far from concluded. However, I suggest that the official guidance provided to teachers presently misrepresents the situation in a number of different respects and engenders the fear that teachers may risk a criminal prosecution brought at the instigation of angry parents who feel that their parental rights have been ignored. Isobel Allen's study in 1987 revealed that 96 per cent of parents questioned thought that schools should provide sex education (Allen 1987, p.172). Such parental support has been confirmed by more recent research (NFER 1994). Of course, parents will not agree as to the appropriate age at which sex education should be provided or the exact content of that education. Exactly how schools will devise sex education programmes is beyond the scope of this chapter, but such programmes will be designed in consultation with many parties including parents where discussions will focus upon the particular needs of the pupils (DFE 1994, para. 22; Holly 1989). In developing the sex education programme the issue of responding to requests for confidential information about contraception from individual pupils could be fully discussed with parents. In the course of this discussion schools ought to emphasise to parents the need to talk to their teenage children about sex and its concomitant responsibilities including contraception. However, it could also be acknowledged that some parents will find it difficult to discuss such matters and that pupils may seek the advice of another adult. The school should inform parents that if approached by an individual pupil for advice on contraception they would discuss with the pupil the benefits of talking through the issue with their parents. Where the pupil refuses to do this, confidential advice would be given if the teacher considers, in the bona fide exercise of their professional judgement, that it is in the best interests of the pupil. However, it should also be pointed out that the advice which teachers will be in a position to give will be limited to directing the pupil to another professional or providing information about methods of contraception to which the pupil already had access.

Finally, it is suggested that engendering within young persons a healthy and responsible attitude to sexual relationships based upon 'respect for themselves and others' and 'sensitivity towards the needs and views of others' (DFE Circular 5/94, 1994, para. 8) requires the same of the adults around them.

Notes

1. *Gillick v West Norfolk and Wisbech Area Health Authority and another* [1986] 1 AC 112 was in fact a civil law case in which Mrs Gillick sought from the court a declaration on the law. The effect of a civil declaration on subsequent criminal proceedings is uncertain. It is clear, however, that a declaration only applies to the facts as stated. As such the reasoning of the House of Lords in *Gillick* would not be binding should a teacher be prosecuted for aiding and abetting an offence contrary to the Sexual Offences Act 1956. The arguments accepted by the majority in *Gillick* would, however, be persuasive in so far as they state the present law as applied to health professionals and indicate the wider policy concerns underlying that conclusion.
2. Kaye Wellings and others found that the oral contraceptive pill, condoms and sterilisation were the methods of contraception most relied upon by the adults in their survey (Wellings and others (1994) p. 327).
3. Douglas (1991) p. 43. As Gillian Douglas explains, the Abortion Act 1967 made lawful abortion available on the NHS, which logically meant that the State also had to ensure the provision of contraceptive services. State provision of both abortion and contraception reflected, to some extent, a change in moral attitudes: Walsh (1980).
4. The question whether a young person under the age of 16 has the legal capacity to give valid consent to contraceptive advice and treatment which includes a medical examination is not of direct relevance to teachers, who will not be in a position to prescribe contraceptives. Whether the provision of such advice and treatment to a young person under the age of 16 without parental consent infringes parental rights is considered in Andrew Bainham's chapter in this volume.

5. Accessories and Abettors Act 1861, s. 8. The *actus reus* of a crime is the conduct or state of affairs which a particular offence prohibits. For criminal liability the accused must be proved to have committed the *actus reus* with the necessary *mens rea* or prohibited state of mind.
6. Compare Smith and Hogan (1992) pp. 56-7, 133-415 and Dennis (1987).
7. The research carried out by Anne Miller found that the majority of respondents who had had their first sexual experience when they were 13, 14 or 15 had that sexual experience with another person within that age range: Miller (1994), paras. 2.5.4.-2.5.5.
8. Wellings and others (1994), p. 42. The survey of 14-and 15-year-olds in schools in the North West of England found that 26 per cent of 14-year-olds, 42 per cent of 15-year-olds and 43 per cent of 16-year-olds had had sexual intercourse: Miller (1994), para. 2.5.2.
9. The main concern of young people seeking advice about contraception will be to avoid an unwanted pregnancy. However, decisions about contraception have to be made in the context not only of avoiding an unwanted pregnancy but also in considering the health risks associated with that method and an awareness that contraceptive protection does not ensure protection against other risks such as sexually transmitted diseases. The oral contraceptive pill is one of the most popular forms of contraception with young people. The survey *Sexual Behaviour in Britain* found that 64.1 per cent of 16-to-24-year-olds had used the oral contraceptive pill in the last year: Wellings (1994), p. 331. Whilst being an effective form of contraception the oral contraceptive carries with it uncertain health risks. Further, whilst the more 'effective' methods may offer protection against pregnancy, only barrier methods offer some protection against sexually transmitted diseases including HIV.

4. Gender, sexuality and sex education

Lois Bibbings, Lecturer in Law, The University of Bristol

Introduction

This chapter focuses upon issues of gender, sexuality and sexual orientation as they relate to the provision of sex education. In addition, in the context of gender and sexual orientation, some consideration is given to educational responses to the risk of the sexual transmission of HIV infection. The overall aim is to raise a number of general concerns in relation to the provision and content of sex education programmes, whilst also considering the potential ambit and implications of the legislation and guidance which currently govern the subject in England and Wales.

Sex education, sexuality, morality and gender

Although the need for sex education for all young people has often been asserted, it is important to recognise that some of the issues raised by school sex education have different implications for each gender. Important examples of this include the provision of information about family planning and contraception which could reduce the likelihood of unplanned pregnancies; indeed, most research supports this view (for example, see Jones and others 1985, Jones and others 1986, Chapter 9, and Gordon and others 1972, p. 22). In this respect the availability and accessibility of such information is most significant for females who risk the possibility of pregnancy and the difficult choices which may ensue. Nevertheless, it is important not to lose sight of the fact that most issues are relevant to females and males; for example, boys and men also need to be aware of the means of both planning/avoiding fatherhood as well as preventing the spread of sexually transmitted diseases. Equally, stereotypical perceptions of gender roles affect, and potentially limit, possible options for both females and males. Thus this section is written with the assumption that the gender implications of school sex education provision cannot be reduced exclusively to women's issues.

From a legal perspective, the provision of education, including sex education, is covered by the rules governing direct or indirect discrimination under the Sex Discrimination Act 1975. Under section 22 of the Act either form of discrimination on grounds of sex is unlawful in certain circumstances, including where discrimination occurs in respect of the 'benefits, facilities and services' provided. As a result, sex discrimination can relate both to the availability of subject choices and the way in which subjects are taught. Thus the provision of different forms of information about sex for girls/young women and boys/young men could potentially constitute a breach of section 22, although it is unlikely that separation of males and females for sex education lessons, and differences in the focus of sex education given to these separate groups, would amount to a breach of the Act.[1]

Among international instruments, the Convention on the Elimination of All Forms of Discrimination Against Women (1979) stipulates the need for equal rights and access to education for women and men (Article 10). The same Article amplifies this basic position to include women's rights to the same teaching materials, curricula, exams and teaching staff together with the elimination of any stereotyped concept of the roles of women and men within the provision of instruction (Article 10(b),(c)). The U.N. Convention on the Rights of the Child 1989 calls on states to ensure that education is provided on the basis of 'equal opportunity' (Article 28(1)). However, this does not necessarily mean that provision given to males and females has to be identical; it merely has to be equivalent or of equal value and quantity.

In the light of this it is perhaps significant that both official and informal sex education continue to focus upon female pupils, who receive more sex education in school and from parents than males do (Allen 1987, pp. 180-181, 204). One study found that boys/young men tended to be more critical of school sex education than girls/young women and that the former often stated that they felt 'left out' (Holland and others 1993, p. 7). For example, young men have complained that a tendency to focus upon biological information causes them to feel marginalised; in particular information about menstruation and reproduction focuses upon females and biological motherhood (*ibid*).

Differences of approach in the sex education provided to men and women, whilst arguably not illegal, are still contentious. Feminist writers have, for example, tended to criticise the fact that sex education classes tend to present and reinforce stereotypical, polarised versions of femininity and masculinity as if they were both biologically determined. In addition, Jean Carabine, in a study of how social policy constructs women's sexuality, states that such policy, when it addresses motherhood or reproduction, often conveys 'implicit messages about biological motherhood as married, heterosexual and of vaginal intercourse as the method of reproduction' (Carabine 1992, p. 33). Similarly, commentators have noted the prominence of notions of 'appropriate' sexuality for women (submissive) and men (dominant) (*ibid*, p. 33, Wolpe 1987, p. 37). AnnMarie Wolpe notes that:

> For the past hundred years, female sexuality and its fulfilment, as defined in terms of middle-class values, have been located within marriage and the bearing of children. Male sexuality, on the other hand, has been represented quite differently, as a primordial urge which must be gratified not necessarily within marriage. (p. 38)

On a more practical level, research has found that young women are particularly affected by repeated emphasis upon their reproductive capacity (Thomson and Scott 1991, p. 7). Similar notions of female sexuality as negative and male sexuality as positive are in fact reflected in young peoples' attitudes. For example, one study of sex education in schools found that oral sex was 'overwhelmingly more often seen as something a girl did to a boy – not the other way around' (Phelps and others 1992, p. 30).

It is also common in the provision of sex education to focus upon women's behaviour as a way of reducing unwanted sexual advances and unplanned pregnancies and postponing sexual experience (Davidson 1990, p. 7). However, whilst this approach is positive in that it stresses the importance of female control it also tends to posit the male as being inherently uncontrollable. Thus, as noted above, men are portrayed as being sexual whilst women are cast as potential victims. One 18-year-old female pupil noticed this tendency in a class and asked the male teacher why, if females can learn to say no, males are unable to do so (Mills 1992, p. 206). Neil Davidson (1990, p.7), in considering masculinity and sex education, notes and criticises this tendency to focus upon the female in order to influence heterosexual sexual behaviour. He argues that men's social and sexual roles and identities are socially constructed and that, therefore, men can also change. Thus concerns about stereotypical representations of men promoted within sex education are as important to recognise as those of women because, as Davidson states:

> ...sex education can present young men with the opportunity to question the assumptions and stereotypes they carry about being men. (*ibid.* p. 8)

Whilst such an approach to sex education would theoretically be possible under current legislation and guidance relating to the basic curriculum, it is probably unlikely to be widely adopted.

The moral context

The reproductive focus of sex education and stereotypical conceptions of gender and gender roles could be reinforced by legislation or guidance which calls for information to be placed firmly in a particular moral context. While all effective sex education would necessarily include the exploration of attitudes and values, including moral values, there has been a growing pressure to develop models of sex education that are moralistic, that is, morally prescriptive. Links between biological information, motherhood, heterosexuality, marriage and reproduction were evident in the debates concerning the moral role and content of school sex education. John Patten's assertion that 'Moral values lie at the heart of education' (*The Times*, 7 December 1993) reflects certain values and prioritises certain conceptions of gender and sexual roles. That morality was a concern of MPs in discussing education policy was also clear from the comments of Patten's Minister of State who reportedly saw the 1994 sex education guidelines as part of the Government's campaign to promote family values (*The Independent*, 2 May 1994).

More specifically, such moralistic models of sex education tend, amongst other things, to advocate specific roles as being natural for women and, hence, potentially encourage limited perceptions of female choice in sexual and other spheres. Similar assertions could be made in relation to the roles of males propounded within such sex education. Although the roles which are being promoted differ, it is still possible to assert that stereotypical and limited conceptions of masculinity are encapsulated in such conceptions of sex education (Holland and others 1993, p. 33). The difference, however, is arguably that men benefit from a society which 'systematically privilege[s] male over female' (*ibid.*). Here heterocentricity is the privileged discourse with the nuclear family, marriage and motherhood posited as normative structures (see generally Carabine 1992). For example, in relation to the provision of school sex education, the 1994 Circular upholds a traditional interpretation of the moral context of sex education:

> Pupils should accordingly be encouraged to appreciate the value of stable family life, marriage and the responsibilities of parenthood. (DFE Circular 1994, paragraph 8)

The Circular is, of course, not binding upon schools but may significantly influence policy and practice. However, section 46 of the Education (No.2) Act 1986 calls on the local education authority, the governing body and the head teacher of a school to take such steps as are reasonably practicable to secure that, where sex education is given, it is given in such a manner as to 'encourage those pupils to have due regard to moral considerations and the value of family life'.

It is evident that moralistic concerns have been incorporated into both legislation and guidance on sex education. Consequently, it is possible, and indeed probable, that certain conceptions of female and male social and sexual roles are more likely to be discussed and deemed acceptable (explicitly or implicitly) than others. However, the separation of the different elements of sex education between the basic curriculum and National Curriculum science, combined with the parental right of withdrawal (discussed below), creates an ironic twist in the context of John Patten's concerns for a moral context to sex education. As Doug McAvoy, General Secretary of the National Union of Teachers, has noted:

> The Education Secretary's plan to give greater emphasis to moral and ethical questions could come to nothing if parents exercise their right to opt pupils out of sex education lessons. (*The Times*, 7 December 1993)

The emphasis placed upon sex education within the context of marriage and stable family life contained in the legislation and guidance can also have the effect of excluding and offending many children and their families whose own experience is very different to this model. For example, this could possibly have a marked effect upon the offspring of single or unmarried, cohabiting mothers who, as women, have tended in recent years to be blamed and castigated for their 'predicament', particularly by the Government and the media. One 16-year-old pupil suffered such confusion:

> My parents aren't married or anything but it never really worried me until this teacher kept on going on about husbands and wives having sex. She made me feel my mum was a prossie. (Mills 1992, p. 210)

Some teachers also acknowledge this problem and recognise the eventual farce which can result, with a teacher extolling the virtues of married life in the full knowledge that many of her or his pupils may have divorced, unmarried, lesbian or gay parents (*ibid*, p. 211 and Darlington (1994), p. 329).

Such difficulties could, however, be mitigated by the 1994 Circular, a fact that also illustrates that the stance of the Department for Education and Employment is not completely consistent in its moralistic concerns. Thus the 1994 Circular, whilst prioritising 'a clear framework of values ... the value of stable family life, marriage and the responsibilities of parenthood' (DFE Circular (1994), paragraph 8), also includes recognition that many people live very differently to the stated ideal and therefore stresses that: 'Teachers need to acknowledge that many children come from backgrounds that do not reflect such values or experiences' (*ibid*). However, it must be assumed that this is by no means intended to detract wholly from the former statement. In consequence, the latter statement presumably marks a minor recognition that 1990s Britain is a pluralistic society, and that in a purportedly democratic state some reference has to be made to those who live lives very different from the aspirations of the Secretary of State. Thus the justification for including this additional guidance is clearly stated as being to avoid 'causing hurt and offence ... and to allow such children to feel a sense of worth' (*ibid*); presumably despite their lesser status in some people's eyes. Nevertheless, such alternative circumstances are not to be advocated; instead, teachers are called upon to help pupils 'whatever their circumstances' to 'raise their sights' (*ibid*). Consequently, if the guidelines are followed closely there remains a danger that some pupils' own experiences and moral standards may be belittled and portrayed as being less acceptable and, by implication, deviant.

Although this consideration for young people whose background does not reflect supposedly traditional moral values may alleviate the situation, arguably it does not go far enough as the core of normative or normalising values remains. Indeed, the Sex Education Forum recommends a very different approach. Ideally, the Forum maintains (in its *Framework* guidance) that, such education should encompass:

> An acceptance and exploration of difference. It is likely that young people will have very different social, cultural, ethnic and religious backgrounds with correspondingly different moral and cultural frameworks. It is important that the value of a range of moral views and choices are explored and shared, including the choice not to be sexually active. (Thomson and Scott 1992)

Initially, it is perhaps significant to note that this document is drafted in extremely wide terms which could be interpreted very differently by opposing interest groups and is consequently potentially weakened. Nevertheless, the wording is also a strength as it has enabled the Framework to be endorsed by a wide variety of organisations including: the Catholic Marriage Advisory Council; the Church of England Board of Education; the Jewish Marriage Council; the Lesbian and Gay Christian movement; the Methodist Church Division of Education and Youth; the National Council of Women of Great Britain; and the National AIDS Trust.

Another conception of an ideal sex education programme has been offered by Helen Lenskyj. In a feminist critique of sex education policies in Canada she states:

> A feminist approach to sex education requires that teachers promote among both male and female students the notion that human sexuality is not, or should not be defined exclusively in male heterosexual terms; that women are developing autonomous sexual identities; and that lesbians and homosexuals are defining their sexuality in fulfilling and responsible ways. Such programmes will of necessity challenge sexism, homophobia and male violence against women and children, and may ultimately bring about a celebration of the difference and diversity within human sexuality. (Lenskyj 1990, pp. 217-8)

This goes further than the Sex Education Forum in that it is more specific and would doubtless not be endorsed by all the organisations which lent their names to *the Framework*. The Forum's statement, however, could be viewed as implying much that is in Lenskyj's model.

Advice on contraception

It is not, however, only the provision of sex education programmes which is important; arguably adolescents (female and male) need the ability to consult teachers on sexual matters outside lessons. This is particularly important given that most young people feel unable to approach their parents. In order for young people to feel that they are able to do this, there must be some form of guarantee of confidentiality. Thus the problems with confidentiality, highlighted by Jo Bridgeman in Chapter 3, could mean that some pupils feel unable to seek support. In particular, the confusion amongst GPs and girls/young women over the decision reached in the Gillick case (*Gillick v West Norfolk and Wisbech Area Health Authority* [1986] AC 112) and its effect upon GPs faced with underage adolescents requesting contraceptives has exacerbated this problem (*The Guardian*, 26 August 1993. See also Holly 1989, p. 19).

To summarise briefly, in 1983 Victoria Gillick brought a legal case against her local health authority to ensure that girls/young women under the age of 16 were not given contraceptive advice by any doctor without their parent's consent. She lost the case in the House of Lords, however, confusion spread about the effect of the decision, which has in some instances caused uncertainty or misconceptions on the part of girls/young women, doctors and even teachers who are asked for advice by their pupils. At present, in maintained secondary schools female pupils who request advice about contraception may, in most cases, seek that information without their parents or others being informed unless an individual is judged to be at risk (see White 1995 Qs. 43,47 and DFE 1994, paragraphs 39,40). Beyond this, recently drafted advice for teachers states that general issues may be discussed with pupils under 16 if they arise as part of teaching and that teachers may provide information on local contraceptive services unless this would be contrary to the school's sex education policy. Specific information may be given about health clinics or medical staff even if the pupil concerned has been withdrawn from sex education (unless school policy states otherwise). However, the legal position of teachers offering contraceptive advice to young people under the age of 16 is unclear, although it is unlikely that a successful prosecution would result especially if the teacher honestly believed at the time that the giving of information was in the best interests of the young person concerned (see White 1995; see also Bainham, Chapter 2 and Bridgeman, Chapter 3, both herein). A draft version of the 1994 Circular included a warning that giving such advice without parental consent could 'amount to a criminal offence' but this was removed from the final version (DFE 1993b, paragraph 38). The 1994 Circular calls for 'particular care' to be exercised in relation to pupils under 16 and states that as a general rule giving individual pupils advice on such matters without parental knowledge or consent would be 'an inappropriate exercise of a teacher's professional responsibility' (DFE 1994, para. 39). However, there is a warning that 'the legal position of a teacher giving advice in such circumstances has never been tested in the courts'. Beyond this, paragraph 40 includes the suggestion that where such individual advice is sought pupils should be encouraged to talk with parents or a health service professional. These issues are analysed in Chapter 2 by Andrew Bainham and Chapter 3 by Jo Bridgeman.

The parental right of withdrawal

Parents may withdraw their children from sex education (other than biological aspects covered under the National Curriculum), without giving any reasons (Education Reform Act 1988, section 17A, inserted by the Education Act 1993). Effectively pupils' wishes are overridden by parental desires which need not be explained or justified. This would appear to conflict with Article 12 of the UN Convention on the Rights of the Child which provides, amongst other things, that:

> State Parties shall assure the child who is capable of forming his or her own views the right to express those views freely in all matters affecting the child, the views of the child being given due weight in accordance with the age and maturity of the child.

However, in practice the power of withdrawal will probably only affect a limited number of young people, as few parents are likely to make use of the new section 17A of the 1988 Act. Nevertheless, it is probable that the withdrawal provision will affect females more than males as one may surmise that it is girls and young women who are more likely to be removed from such tuition precisely because of prevailing attitudes to female identity and sexuality. A further concern is that the power of withdrawal could conceivably be exploited by parents who sexually abuse their offspring in an attempt to prevent discovery.

Sexual orientation and sex education

Lesbian and gay sexuality are often not considered, or are considered less favourably, within school sex education. There are a number of possible reasons for this tendency. Ideologies of heterosexuality are explicitly or implicitly present both within society and within the legislation and guidelines relating to sex education and other areas of social policy. Furthermore, homophobic attitudes are prevalent in a society where the age of consent for gay male and heterosexual penetrative sex differs and AIDS is sometimes described as a 'homosexual plague'. In addition, within schools, discussions of homosexuality may be silenced or restricted for various reasons: teachers may be embarrassed, fear media scandals or parental complaints, or may avoid discussion of gay male penetrative sex because such activity is illegal where a participant is under the age of 18 (see Sexual Offences Act 1956 s. 1 as amended by Criminal Justice and Public Order Act 1994, s. 145(1)). Some of these issues will be briefly discussed within this section.

The centrality of heterosexual ideology within social policy and more specifically, sex education policy has been mentioned previously. Social policy, enforced through legislation, can be seen as a means of attempting to regulate sexuality. For example, section 28 Local Government Act 1988, which inserted a new section 2A into the Local Government Act 1986, provides in part that:

(1) A local authority shall not –
(a) intentionally promote homosexuality or publish material with the intention of promoting homosexuality;
(b) promote the teaching in any maintained school of the acceptability of homosexuality as a pretended family relationship;...
(2) Nothing in subsection (1) above shall be taken to prohibit the doing of anything for the purpose of treating or preventing the spread of disease[2].

The 1988 Act reflects negative views of lesbians and gay men. This has been displayed by the Conservative Government's emphasis upon the heterosexual family and such family values during the late 1980s and into the 1990s (see Thomas 1993). This was, and is, reinforced by public concern about the spread of HIV/AIDS, which has been linked to, and sometimes even blamed upon, gay men. However, the section does not prevent teachers from discussing lesbian and gay sexuality; a Department of the Environment Circular issued with the enactment of section 28 states that:

> Section 28 does not affect the activities of school governors, nor of teachers. It will not prevent the objective discussion of homosexuality in the classroom, nor the counselling of pupils concerned about their sexuality. Such activities will continue to be governed by Section 46 of the Education (No. 2) Act 1986 (DoE Circular 12/88, para 20) (NB s.46 promotes a moral context to sex education: see above).

Despite this, a number of commentators and studies suggest that some teachers have been over cautious when providing information about lesbian and gay sexuality. This may, in part, be caused by misconceptions about the applicability of section 28 to schools. Thus a tendency towards self-censorship has been identified (see Thomson and Scott 1992, p. 15). Indeed one teacher reports that section 28 has cast a shadow over discussions in class (Mills 1992, p. 207). Similarly, Martin Stafford (1988) has noted a difficulty associated with presenting positive images of lesbians and gay men or of fully discussing sexual orientation in classrooms.

In the past, the legislation and guidelines relating to sex education have taken a similar, but less overt, approach in relation to sexual orientation to that adopted within section 28. In the 1987 Circular (para 22) (which has been superseded by the 1994 guidance) there was no attempt to proscribe coverage of homosexuality in sex education, but schools were advised that for some people such coverage could cause 'deep offence'. In addition, it stated that:

> There is no place in any school for teaching which advocates homosexual behaviour, which presents it as a norm, or which encourages homosexual experimentation by pupils (DES 1987, para 22).

Thus it is likely that teachers were reluctant or cautious when it came to talking about sexual orientation.

Lesbian and gay experiences of sex education before the 1994 changes reflect this view. In one study of gay male pupils' experiences in schools it was observed in relation to sex education that:

> The students became aware of the underlying dominant ideologies that structured their schooling. They described the narrow range of topics that were discussed in lessons and the overt and covert moral values that were transmitted within the context of normative/prescriptive accounts of the two-parent nuclear family lifestyle. (Mac An Ghaill 1991, p. 295)

They also talked about the focus upon heterosexual experience and procreation and the portrayal of traditional roles for men and women (*ibid* pp. 295-6). The comments of one teacher at a girls' state school reinforces this picture of marginalisation:

> We have a book-box of non-curriculum books which pupils can borrow. In it I've put Annie on My Mind [Nancy Garden, 1988] and some Judy Blume novels which deal with lesbianism. I don't ever bring the subject up but feel I have to wait until they do. (Mills 1992 p. 208)

The 1994 Circular does not include any specific mention of homosexuality but merely states the legal position as regards section 28 and the altered age of consent for gay males (Annex A and Annex B respectively). Indeed, as Neville Harris argues in Chapter 1, given the right of withdrawal of a pupil from sex education, it could be argued that there is less pressure on teachers to omit information on lesbian and gay sexuality from sex education, provided parents are informed of this in advance. However, given both the 1994 Circular's stress on morality, family values, marriage and reproduction, and the continued existence of section 28, it is still likely that such discussions will be limited and largely negative in character; being lesbian or gay will probably not be presented as being normal (see Lind and Butler's view 1995, pp. 5-7). However, the pressure group, Outrage, reportedly saw a glimmer of hope in paragraph 8 of the 1994 Circular, which stresses the need for teachers to acknowledge that whilst sex education should be taught in the context of heterosexual marriage and reproduction, many children come from very different backgrounds and therefore efforts should be made to avoid 'causing hurt and offence ... and to allow such children to feel a sense of worth.'

The absence of positive images of lesbians and gay men as people, sexual partners or parents coupled with a general failure to address homophobia could present an extremely negative perspective to pupils. This could prove particularly disturbing for lesbian and gay pupils who are marginalised, miss out on relevant sex education and thus, in practice, may fail to receive education which promotes their full development as adults. This latter point could mean that lesbian and gay pupils do not receive equal respect for their rights to education under international human rights documents and that they are not truly receiving education which will 'promote the ... mental and physical development of pupils' and prepare them for the 'experiences of adult life' (Education Reform Act 1988, section 1; see Lind and Butler 1995, pp. 5-7 and the U.N. Convention on the Rights of the Child, articles 28, 29). Indeed one pupil stressed the need for homosexuality to be addressed within schools as 'no other info [sic] which I received had any relevance towards my sexuality...' (Thomson and Scott 1991, p. 8). Equally, silences or brief consideration of such issues can encourage or feed the prejudices of heterosexual pupils and fail to prepare them 'for an adult world they will share with homosexuals' (Lind and Butler 1995, p. 5). Yet what are the effects of teaching and discussing homosexuality in a more positive light? Research indicates that human sexuality courses do increase pupils' tolerance towards the practices of others but have little effect upon the pupils' individual sexual behaviour (Adame 1985, p. 9). Thus teaching about alternative sexual orientations would, most probably, have an insignificant effect upon an individual's orientation.

A further area of concern relates to lesbian and, in particular, gay male pupils who seek confidential advice from teachers. There are two major issues here. First, can confidentiality be guaranteed? Lind and Butler (1995, p. 7) have noted that a breach of trust in such circumstances could be severely damaging to the young person concerned. The 1994 Circular suggests that a teacher 'should' inform the head teacher if the teacher believes that 'the pupil has embarked upon or is contemplating, a course of conduct which is likely to place him or her at moral or physical risk or in breach of the law' (DFE 1994, para 40). Thus, where a gay male pupil under the age of 18 is the subject of such a belief, this may cause this course of action to be considered. Beyond this schools should have a policy on confidentiality which may offer guidance.

Secondly, it is theoretically possible that a teacher may face criminal charges in relation to advice given to an under-age gay male. The position here is uncertain given that the guidance on confidentiality has centred around the giving of contraceptive advice to girls/young women under the age of 16 (see section Advice on contraception' and Lind and Butler 1995, p. 7 and DFE 1994, paragraph 40). (Confidentiality is discussed by Jo Bridgeman in Chapter 3.)

Education about HIV/AIDS[3]

Research on HIV/AIDS and children has confirmed that the need for HIV/AIDS education for the young is great (Honigsbaum 1991). This is supported by evidence that growing numbers of young people are HIV positive or have AIDS (PHLS AIDS Centre 1994). The World Health Organisation has estimated that more than 1.5 million children will have been infected with HIV since the beginning of the pandemic in the late 1970s to early 1980s (WHO 1995) and that by the end of the decade 10 million children will have AIDS and another 10 million will have been orphaned by HIV (cited by Margaret Jay in Honigsbaum 1991, Foreword p. ix). Young people, therefore, must be educated to take preventative action both to protect themselves and to safeguard future generations. Thus education about HIV/AIDS should be provided for all pupils (Wight 1993, p. 479). The provision of information for and about high risk activities, is imperative. Consequently, sex education should include information about certain sexual practices and intravenous drug use. In addition, such tuition should attempt to avoid legitimating homophobic prejudices; thus a sex education programme which also addresses such attitudes would be doubly effective (see Lenskyj 1990, pp. 217-8).

The need for full HIV/AIDS education is especially important given that studies suggest that without adequate sex education ignorance will, in most cases, be supplemented by snatches of information, misinformation and myths gleaned from television, films and from other young people (Lees 1994 p. 284; Phelps and others 1992 give examples of such misconceptions). This is especially true in relation to HIV/AIDS. John Balding and David Regis (1991, p.13) quote an extreme example of information from the media which could cause a dangerous sense of complacency amongst the heterosexual population. *The Sun* on 17 November 1990 carried the headline 'Straight Sex Cannot Give You AIDS – Official'; beneath, the paper stated:

> ...the risk of catching AIDS if you are heterosexual is 'statistically invisible'. In other words impossible. So now we know – anything else is just homosexual propaganda.

Such statements, coupled with the understandable tendency to focus upon 'high risk groups', can encourage a false sense of security and a blinkered attitude. Phelps, Mellanby and Tripp report such attitudes in a survey of adolescent sexual knowledge amongst 13- and 14-year-olds; they cite one view: 'there is no AIDS round here' (Phelps and others 1992, p. 30). Yet the risk of heterosexual transmission does exist, although it is at present low in the UK (see Holland and others 1990, p. 127). In fact, the risk is arguably greatest for heterosexual women. The Commission of European Communities in 1991 found that women were twice as vulnerable as men to HIV through vaginal intercourse in the absence of other related factors, although the risk of such transmission during unprotected heterosexual penetrative intercourse is statistically low (Commission of the European Communities 1991).[4] In addition, in England current projections on HIV/AIDS in England and Wales suggest that the proportion of seropositive women to men is likely to increase steadily (OPCS Monitor 1991). At least one young woman has recognised the dangers:

> It does frighten me, it really does frighten me because, well really, we are the group that are going to be growing up with this hanging over them. We're going to have to have kids through this. (Holland and others 1990, p. 125)

Despite this, sex education about HIV/AIDS in schools is affected by the same fears associated with other sexual information. Dr Michael Merson, Director of the WHO's Global Programme on AIDS, has warned that 'The belief that sex and AIDS education may encourage sexual activity in young people is a powerful barrier to the introduction of HIV prevention programmes for youth' (*The Guardian*, 1 December 1993). Anne Weyman, Chair of the Sex Education Forum, stressed the dangers of denying young people such information: 'To deny young people this...is to put them at risk of serious mental and physical consequences' (Weyman 1993, p. 3) and the WHO (1995) has also expressed a similar view. The definition of sex education under the Education Act 1993 (s.241(2)) refers specifically to HIV/AIDS and other sexually transmitted diseases. Yet education about AIDS and other sexually-transmitted diseases now forms part of the basic curriculum sex education, rather than National Curriculum biological information. This means that parents can withdraw their offspring from

HIV/AIDS instruction. This would not be problematic if, in all such instances, parents provided full and accurate information about HIV/AIDS themselves; however, it would be erroneous to assume that this is the case.

Conclusion

The subjects of gender, sexuality and sexual orientation raise a number of issues in relation to the provision of sex education in schools. It is argued here that underlying the concerns is the need for comprehensive sex education for all children and young people. The legislation and guidelines regarding the content of sex education and the context in which any sex related information is conveyed affect the achievement of this goal – as does the possibility of parental removal of offspring from such instruction within the basic curriculum. This latter right could potentially undermine the ideal of sex education for all. Whilst the withdrawal provisions arguably allow for the recognition of religious freedom and personal choice in relation to parents and families, the ability of parents to withdraw their offspring theoretically represents one of the most problematic effects of recent changes in sex education policy.

In the light of these concerns it is perhaps significant that the United Nations Committee on Rights of the Child, which examined the existence of children's rights in Britain under the Convention on the Rights of the Child, levelled criticisms at the UK in relation to the provision of health education for young people. One criticism related to the right of parental withdrawal from basic curriculum sex education in schools and the general absence of any right of the child to express her/his opinions (UN Committee on Rights of The Child 1995, paragraph C:14). In addition, the Committee recommended that, in relation to 'the problem of teenage pregnancy', prevention orientated education programmes should be introduced (*ibid.*, paragraph D:30).

To conclude, it is argued that sex education should follow the pluralistic approach advocated in the Sex Education Forum's *Framework* provided it is interpreted in a fairly liberal manner. However, this document is drafted in broad terms and a number of interpretations are possible. I am arguing that sex education should ideally be provided for all within schools. Consequently, the power of parental withdrawal should be removed or limited to instances where parents can give good and specific reasons for their objections and where their offspring do not object (such an objection could at present potentially be considered within an application under section 8 of the Children Act 1989 for a 'specific issue order' but may not always defeat the parental power). Thus some account could be taken of genuine religious or other objections to be respected and followed, whilst, at the same time, young people could also be given a say as to their education in sexual matters. Further, I would argue that the information provided and the issues discussed in sex education should, as far as possible, be wide ranging; neither promoting nor condemning lesbians, gay men, single parents or those who live in 'non-traditional' family units. Rather, such instruction should reflect and describe the diversity of sexual experiences and relationships within contemporary Britain and the plurality of opinions relating to these experiences.

Education should also try to avoid stereotypical conceptions of women and female sexuality and of men and male sexuality; and it should provide comprehensive information about HIV/AIDS and other sexually transmitted diseases. Teachers (or perhaps for every school, at least one teacher) should receive specific training in relation to these matters and should be offered guidance as to possible responses to pupils' questions. Queries and 'precocious' questions should be treated confidentially unless the circumstances appear particularly serious and pupils should be made aware of the possibility that confidences could be breached.[5] Pupils should, additionally, be encouraged to talk about the issues in general terms within class and with potential and actual sexual partners. In addition, communication may be aided by peer group learning programmes in which there is at least some facility for young people to help teach each other and/or discuss the issues (see WHO 1994, p. 77).

Most significantly, sex education programmes should be constructed and taught with an awareness that no such programme can be value free, even if it takes place in science lessons (Thomson 1993, p. 11). For example, gender roles, morality and notions of normality are conveyed, explicitly or implicitly, through such education. As a result, 'Teachers need to be aware of the hidden values implicit in many sex education materials and approaches and to make these values explicit' (*ibid*).

Notes

1. For more detail in relation to the impact of the 1975 Act on education see Harris (1995), pp. 217-220. For a general discussion of the Sex Discrimination Act 1975 see Feldman 1993, pp. 879-886.

2. For a description of the history of the legislation and its aims see Thomas and Costigan (1990), pp. 8-9.
3. This chapter focuses upon HIV/AIDS education; however, it is recognised that such information must not completely overwhelm awareness of sexually transmitted diseases like chlamydia, gonorrhoea and syphilis.
4. For information on women HIV/AIDS and the risks of HIV transmission for heterosexual women see WHO (1994), Chapter 15; Doyal (1994); and Panos Dossier 4 (1990), Chapter 1.
5. Currently precocious questions raised by a pupil may cause a teacher to inform parents, as may suspicions that a pupil may be in breach of the law or at moral risk: DFE (1994), paragraph 40.

5. Ethnicity, religion and sex education

Anthony Bradney, Senior Lecturer in Law, The University of Leicester

Introduction

Great Britain is a largely secular society within which religious minorities seek to secure a place. It is also a multi-cultural country where relatively small ethnic minority communities come to terms with a social structure historically based on assumptions of cultural homogeneity. Understanding these facts is an essential precondition to understanding the law relating to sex education. Understanding the effect the law can have on ethnic and religious minorities is, in itself, a precondition for understanding the impact of the law taken as a whole.

Eighty per cent of the population engage in no regular form of worship (Central Statistical Office 1995, p. 222). For these people religion is, at most, a nominal matter involving no more than occasional declarations of church membership on official and unofficial documents. It is true that British social life shows vestigial traces of Great Britain's Christian heritage. For example, the special place of Sunday in the working week, the dates of many public holidays and the fact (in England and Scotland) of the legal establishment of a Christian church all attest to the religious past of the country. Such things are, however, precisely matters of the past. Religion now has little significance in either the public consciousness or the political life of the nation. This is something acknowledged, if lamented, as much by religious bodies themselves as by anyone else. Thus, for example, when the Christian churches sought to oppose the recent changes to Sunday trading legislation they argued on the ground of 'the human need to preserve one day a week as a day different from others' not on the ground of the sacred nature of Sunday (Auld 1984, paragraph 11).

For 20 per cent of the population, however, the position is different. Regular religious worship is part of their lives and, for some of these people, religion is central to their sense of identity. It is easy to underestimate the differences between those who are religious and those who are not. For those who are not religious, religion can seem to be merely a cultural matter, a facet of someone's life. It is seen as being voluntary and peripheral to personal identity. Religion is just one of many things which identifies you as a member of a group you have chosen to join: '[O]ne sometimes gets the feeling that religion is like stamp-collecting or playing squash, a minor hobby' (Knott 1986, p. 4). However, as Dummett (1986, p. 12-13) notes, for those who are religious, religion is obligatory and given. Joining a religious group is a reaction to a person's perception of the state of nature. One is a Muslim because there is Allah, a Christian because there is God. Your religion has in this sense chosen you. The imperatives of one's religion therefore take priority over any other command including the law of the state.

Religion is often confused with ethnicity. In fact there will often be a great overlap between examples of the two concepts. However, they are not synonyms. Thus, for example, many Christians in Great Britain are from the white indigenous population, but not all of them are. There are Chinese, Indian and African-Caribbean Christian churches, to name but a few. Equally, within Great Britain, Muslims are most frequently drawn from ethnic groups not indigenous to Great Britain. Yet there are also the Muslims who come from the indigenous population. More importantly, even where ethnicity and religion overlap, religion may have priority in identity. People may see themselves as Christian rather than Tamil or Chinese, Muslim rather than British or Pakistani (Knott and Khokker 1993). Yet ethnic origin can, in itself, be a separate source of identity. Ethnicity, either at a specific level of religion (for example Gujarati) or at a more general level (for example, Asian) can serve as a focus for construction of self (Modood 1988).

Given the prevailing political ideology in Great Britain, people's sense of religious or ethnic identity should be both important and at the same time irrelevant in the structure of British society. Politically and philosophically, Great Britain is a liberal democracy. Liberal societies do not interfere in their citizens' selection of their personal values: '[T]he [liberal] state is not to do anything intended to favour or promote any particular comprehensive doctrine rather than another, not to give greater assistance to those who pursue it' (Rawls 1988, p. 262). It therefore follows that liberal states should be silent on matters of ethnic identity and religious affiliation, thus recognising the irrelevance to the state of these matters, whilst allowing individuals within the state to make their own choices about identity and thereby recognising the importance to individuals of these things. This silence or neutrality is most usually debated in terms of the liberal state's attitudes towards religion:

> One may say that the law-religion relationship is a natural locus of the liberal neutrality. The idea of a secular liberal state, i.e. the state which neither gets involved in matters religious nor inhibits in any way religious expression and activities has long been understood as best encapsulated by the idea of the state's neutrality towards religion. (Sadurski 1990, p. 167)

From this it follows that '[a]mong those things which are held to be self-evident in British society is the principle that there should be no coercion in matters of religion' (*The Times*, 14 August 1984). Individuals should neither be forced into a particular religion nor prevented from practising their religion. The state should only coerce people in matters of religion where an individual's religion directly harms another. The law and the courts should be '... perfectly impartial in matters of religion'[1].

In so far as ethnic identity constitutes a value system these arguments are equally valid. Choice of ethnic identity is, following liberal principles, a personal choice in which the state has no warrant to interfere. The state cannot justifiably impose laws upon people which involve them giving up their ethnic identities unless the expression of their identities conflicts with the same rights enjoyed by other people.

Great Britain is a signatory both to the United Nations Declaration of Human Rights and the European Convention on Human Rights. In so being it accepts obligations to protect both its ethnic and religious minorities. In many countries the general rights which arise because of this neutrality are protected under the state's constitution. This is not so in Great Britain. This follows from the unwritten nature of the British Constitution. Freedoms, rights and liberties in Great Britain are protected by the cumulative result of general legislation and by the general principle that one is free to do whatever is not prohibited by the law.

For ethnic minorities the main source of protection under British law is the Race Relations Act 1976. How effective that legislation is, is open to question (Gregory 1987). It does, however, at the very least, provide rhetorical support for the idea of the equal value of each person no matter what their ethnic background. British law does not afford to religion the same protection that it does to matters of ethnicity. There is no general legislation analogous to the Race Relations Act 1976. Instead, specific laws seek to address themselves to the particular needs of religious minorities. These are either intended to resolve conflicts with the legal system which occur because of social practices arising from religious beliefs or to facilitate the believer's fulfilment of their civil obligations. Thus the Motor-cycle Crash-Helmets (Religious Exemption) Act 1976 permits Sikhs not to wear crash-helmets and various parts of the Marriage Acts 1949 to 1990 allow people to marry in a religious and civil service at the same time. Whether the cumulative effect of this legislation is the neutrality towards religion that is sought, and whether that neutrality is in fact desirable, is open to question (Bradney 1993).

The current law relating to sex education attempts to accommodate the ethnic and religious sensibilities of minorities in a way that is similar to other legislation that deals with specifically religious needs. Following the passage of the Education Act 1993, it insists on mandatory provision of sex education in maintained schools, but allows parents to withdraw their children from such education. How far the law is successful in meeting needs, and how far it would be desirable for it to meet such needs, is, as will be seen, debatable.

Sex, health and morality

Education about sex cannot be seen in isolation from the educational process generally. It forms part of both of the more general areas of moral and health education. It is thus understandable that the Government's advice to schools writing a syllabus for sex education directs the school's attention to National Curriculum Council publications on these areas (DFE 1994, paragraph 19). These documents[2] pay rather mixed regard to questions of the ethnic origins and religious sensibilities of pupils and parents.

In *Spiritual and Moral Development – A Discussion Paper*, religion is given early consideration and schools are told that they should be aware of the religious background of their pupils and sensitive in their response to pupils who have a religious faith (at p.6). In *Curriculum Guidance 5: Health Education*, whilst the question of pupil's ethnic background is raised at the beginning of the paper, religion is given only a cursory reference towards the end of the discussion (pp.2 and 29). In *Curriculum Guidance 8: Education for Citizenship*, although it is said that 'This component...increases awareness of and works towards resolving some of the tensions and conflicts that occur between groups which perceive each other to be socially, racially, ethnically or culturally different' (at p.6), no mention is made of religious divides. Ethnicity is seen as being of much greater import than religion. This failure to perceive religious identity as being a matter of significance is mirrored in the Government's own notes of guidance which do not explicitly address this question (DFE Circular 5/94 1994).

This refusal to highlight the question of religion is surprising in the light of the genesis of the current legal provisions relating to sex education.

The growth of sex education

The number of schools including sex education in their curriculum grew through the 1970s and 1980s (Massey 1990, p. 134). It first became mandatory for schools to consider offering sex education with the passage of section 18 of the Education (No.2) Act 1986. The introduction of this requirement in the original Bill, according to a written answer given by the Minister responsible, Angela Rumbold, prompted 350 written objections (H.C Debs, Volume 102, column 769w). The likelihood that parents would object to sex education on religious grounds was raised in debate (*ibid,* column 1091). However, the Government rejected the suggestion that parents should be allowed to withdraw their children from such classes, stating that '[p]upils' education would be seriously harmed if parents had an absolute right to withdraw their children ...' (*ibid*, column 1057).

The scale of complaints about sex education after the passage of the 1986 Act is impossible to measure accurately and can only be estimated from those few incidents that found their way into the press or academic literature. Harris, in his report on the working of section 23 of the Education Reform Act 1988, which allows parents to complain about the operation of the curriculum of a school, noted one complaint where a Christian parent wished to withdraw a child from lessons on sex education (Harris 1992, pp. 87–90). *The Guardian* reported a separate incident although on this occasion no formal complaint was made (*The Guardian*, 22 June 1993). Another case is referred to by Robinson in his account of changes to education law (Robinson 1992, p. 1191). The number of these reports is likely to underestimate the size of the problem. There is a failure to provide a formal mechanism for complaints specifically about sex education and the complexity of the general section 23 procedure has meant that parents are ignorant of that procedure, resulting in such incidents coming to public notice in an ad hoc manner. All this conspires to mean that their final total is likely to under-represent the degree of parent or pupil dissatisfaction with sex education.

A different indication of dissatisfaction with the content of the 1986 Act as regards sex education can be gained from reading literature produced by religious bodies. Some of this is firmly opposed to sex education. Thus McDermott and Ahsan (1986, p.47) note that 'at a recent Muslim Teachers' Association Conference for both parents and teachers, the general view of the parents was solidly against sex education in schools'. Other publications do not totally reject sex education but take a cautious approach to both the way in which it is taught and to its content (Sarwar 1994, pp. 9-11). Such publications are in accord with a general attitude common in religious and ethnic minorities which sees British state education as both providing possible material advantages for children and being likely to compromise the religious and community values of pupils (Helweg 1979, p.110).

The right of parental objection

The passage of the Education Act 1993 gave the Government the opportunity to reconsider its attitude to sex education. In response to back-bench pressure in the House of Lords, Baroness Blatch, on behalf of the Government, announced that henceforth 'parents should have the right to withdraw their children from sex education in much the same way as they have the right at present to withdraw them from religious education' (H.L. Debs, Volume 547, column 139). This change, which became section 17A of the Education Reform Act 1988, was described in the media as a 'concession to fundamentalist religious groups' (*The Guardian*, 22 June 1993). Baroness Blatch herself said that although debate had turned only on the needs of those objecting on religious grounds, the right of parental objection was intended to apply to all parents with 'strongly held beliefs' (H.L. Debs, Volume 547, column 140). Notwithstanding this comment, the new right of parental objection greatly strengthens the position of religious and ethnic minority communities who wish to bring up their children in a traditional value system.

Possible reasons for objection

Future objections to sex education, leading to withdrawal of children, are likely to centre on two matters: first, the way in which sex education is taught; and, secondly, the content of that which is taught.

Objections are likely to be based on different cultural notions of modesty and honour. Some parents are likely to object if sex education is not taught to single sex classes and if those teaching sex education classes are not of the same sex as their pupils (IQRA 1991, p. 18; Muslim Parliament 1992, p. 21). However, objections to the delivery of sex education are likely to go further than attention to the sex of the teachers. Some parents may object to 'graphic illustrations of sexual organs and sex play' (McDermott and Ahsan 1986, p. 46). The use of drama and role play is seen as being one way of providing a greater depth of learning in sex education (Blakey and Pullen 1991). Such a method is likely to be regarded by some as being objectionable if it involves the pupils taking part in, or possibly even seeing, events which are not permitted within the minority culture. The project described by Blakey and Pullen, for example, involved, amongst other things, a 16th birthday party where parents were not present (*ibid.*, p. 161). It has long been accepted that in general '[t]heoretically, health education materials should be language and culture specific' (Bhopal and Donaldson 1988, p. 140). However, objections have already been raised by religious groups about bi-lingual sex education literature 'because Urdu, Punjabi and to a lesser extent Arabic, lack an uncontroversial and value-free vocabulary ...' (Muslim Parliament 1992), p. 22).

Content is likely to provide even greater difficulties than delivery. The original 1986 legislation laid down that sex education had to be given 'in such a manner as to encourage ... pupils to have due regard to moral considerations and the value of family life' (s.46 Education (No. 2) Act 1986). The content of sex education according to the Government's own advice should 'not be value-free' (DFE 1994, para. 8). Objective sex education, if such a thing were possible, would not comply with the statutory framework. However, it is difficult to arrive at a heuristic framework within which to teach children moral education without offending religious or cultural feelings. Work has been done by the Sex Education Forum to try and arrive at materials which present a range of ethnic and religious perspectives on issues raised in sex education (Thomson 1993). However, the deep-rooted difficulties raised in this area can be illustrated by one simple example. Key stage 3 of the National Curriculum Council's guidance on health education says that at this stage children should have learnt 'that people have a right not to be sexually active; recognise that parenthood is a matter of choice' (National Curriculum Council 1990a, p. 16). For some religions marriage is obligatory and sexual activity a compulsory part of marriage (Bradney 1993, p. 39).

Attitudes towards sex education may reflect not just different conclusions about what is best for the individual needs of the pupil but wholly different starting points about how one reasons about questions of this kind. Liberalism rests on an ontology of the individual. Many religions, including some forms of Christianity, treat the religious community itself as the base unit (*ibid*, p. 27). Complaints about sex education may reflect deeper concerns than matters relating to notions of modesty or behaviour appropriate for the different sexes, important as these are. In other areas of law there has already been conflict between the essentially Aristotelian approach of British education, which centres on the child as an individual learner and seeks to develop her or his best talents, and the communitarian nature of some ethnic minority cultures and some religions which sees the child primarily as a bearer of that culture of that religion (Bradney 1987). This problem is likely to recur in the context of a form of sex education which sees its mission thus:

> The goal of sex education should be to promote sexual health. The person who is sexually healthy has considered and reflected on their options and made choices in the light of those considerations and reflections. (Massey 1990, p. 138)

Any attempt to make an individual child think about the importance of sex in their personal lives is likely to conflict with a religion or ethnic community which holds itself out as knowing what the position of sex should be in that child's life.

Predicting which kind of activities or what type of content will offend particular parents is impossible. No religion presents a monolithic face to sex education. Each religion is infected with divisions which reflect both schismatic theological tendencies and the effect of ethnic culture on religious belief. Thus, for example, the question of the role of women in society, which is a central issue in sex education, is, for Muslims, as much a matter of ethnic background as a particular reading of the Koran and the Hadith (Jeffrey 1979, Chapter 1). Equally, individuals from the same ethnic background may hold different views about sex education depending on their education, social class or age.

Children, communities and parents

The legal position established for sex education following the passage of the Education Act 1993 is one which is inherently contradictory, owing its existence more to pragmatic politics than to any attempt to construct a coherent system.

The initial position adopted by the Government in 1986 was that sex education was something that was desirable for a child. The strength of this position is that it treats children as human beings who have individual needs and whose needs must be protected by Government. Using this framework following traditional liberal arguments children were treated as people who make choices. The weakness of this position is that it ignores the fact that traditionally liberals have not treated children as people. Historically, for liberals, children, like the insane, were normally lesser beings needing the protection of others (Mill 1972, p. 73). For this reason, under British law parents are allowed a general licence to bring up children in the way they think fit. A parent who withdraws their child from school at 16, even though the child is intellectually capable of continuing and the parent financially capable of supporting them, incurs no legal penalty. The law sets minimum standards but, in the main, treats, the child as the creature of the parent.

At the same time that the original 1986 Act ignored the traditional role of the parent, it also ignored the argument that 'like individuals, communities can only flourish under propitious circumstances. They need a sense of their own worth…' (Parekh 1990, p. 72). If religious groups and ethnic minorities are best to replicate themselves they must be able to bring up their children in their own way. Bringing up your children in a particular manner can be both an expression of religious belief and a reflection of ethnic identity.

The change in the 1993 Education Act involves copying the position of parents with respect to religious education. On the one hand the Government decided that religious education is a necessary facet of any child's education by making it part of the basic curriculum (s.2(1)(a) Education Reform Act 1988). Having done that it then gave parents a right to withdraw their children from lessons if they objected to such education (s.9(3) Education Reform Act 1988). In both the case of religious education and sex education the Government's acceptance of the privileged position of parents was the result of considerable back-bench pressure prompting the Government in the case of religious education to accept amendments that were introduced and in the case of sex education to introduce amendments of its own. In relation to sex education the Government went further than it had done in the case of religious education in its advice to schools:

> The teaching offered by schools should be complementary and supportive to the role of parents, and should have regard to parents' views

> about its content and presentation. (DFE 1994, paragraph 7)
>
> In discharging their duties relating to sex education, governors ... are ... required to have regard to any representations made to them by anyone connected with the community served by the school .... (*ibid*, paragraph 18)

However, this attitude towards parents in education law conflicts with the treatment of the respective importance of the views of children and parents in other areas of law. In family law generally the views of children, as compared with the wishes of parents, have achieved an increasing importance (as noted by Andrew Bainham in Chapter 2). In the influential decision of *Gillick v West Norfolk and Wisbech Area Health Authority* ([1986] 1 AC 112) it was said that greater and greater attention should be paid to the views of a child as it grew older. In relation to education, when determining custody issues, the courts have specifically noted the need to take into account the wishes of the older child (*Re S* [1992] 2 FLR 313). Children may now, under section 8 of the Children Act 1989, 'divorce' their parents and take legal action on their own initiative to separate themselves from their parents' actual and legal custody (Houghton-James, 1994). Decisions made under the Children Act 1989 are determined, under section 1(1), according to the court's perception of the child's best interests. They do not rest on the needs of the parent or the community to which the child belongs. Whilst this perception of the child's autonomy which underlies much of family law might justify a right for the child to withdraw from sex education lessons, it is at odds with a parent's right to withdraw their children (see Chapter 2 by Andrew Bainham).

Conclusion

The Education Act 1993 has created an inherently unstable situation. Teachers are both required to pay attention to the educational needs of the individual child and to the wishes of parents and communities in a context where these matters will, inevitably, come into conflict. Rather than seeking to determine the appropriate balance between the respective rights of the parties involved, the Government has created a system which devolves decisions down to a local level. Under such a structure accommodations made will reflect very specific issues in local politics and the personal relations between individual teachers and parents. This is likely to mean that the provision of sex education will vary greatly from area to area as teachers seek to cope with the wishes of parents in their particular schools. Since parents have an absolute right to withdraw children from sex education lessons the balance of power lies with them. Arrangements made in one year in order to gain one group of parents' consent to sex education may need to be completely altered in another year for a different group of parents. In a school serving a multi-religious and multi-ethnic community there may be widespread differences in what various parents will accept in terms of the delivery and content of sex education.

The root cause of this instability in the law relating to sex education lies in the more general failure in British politics to think through a coherent approach to questions of ethnicity and religion. An acknowledgement of previous widespread unjustifiable discriminatory attitudes towards religious and ethnic minorities can result in a failure to address the question of the boundaries of permissible behaviour in a liberal democracy. Ethnicity and religion are treated at times not just as having value but as having absolute value in themselves. Ethnicity or religious belief becomes a trump which will defeat any other argument. However, although a liberal democracy is debarred from choosing values for its members, at the same time, like any other political theory, it must hold fast to its own claims to truth (Dworkin 1984, p. 155). If children are members of a society, and if sex education is a necessary part of children's education, where that education is directed towards making them full participatory members of the society, then, in a liberal state, no parental right to object is permissible. This liberal idea of rights conflicts directly with the value systems of some ethnic and religious minorities (Mawdudi 1980). Its application will cause offence to some parents and pupils. To act in any other way, however, results in the present volatile and precarious position.

The strong stance advocated above can only be justified if a number of prior conditions are met. First, sex education must in fact be necessary for a child's full participation in society. Secondly, the state must act in an even-handed manner, enforcing its demands on all parents in all situations where the child's needs are not in accord with the parent's wishes. Thirdly, the state must not fail to meet the legitimate needs of ethnic or religious minorities. Whether all of these conditions are found in practice is debatable. Sex education may be important for a child but whether it is vital is less clear. The fact that its general provision is of relatively recent origin might suggest that children can in fact participate in society without such education. It is even less clear that the state acts in an even-handed manner when interfering with parental decisions. Notwithstanding the increasing judicial and statutory recognition of infant autonomy the general pattern of family law remains one of non-intervention in what is seen as the essentially private matter of family life (O'Donovan 1985). There is some evidence to suggest that when interventions are made they are more likely to be made in the case of minority families, simply because the family does come from a minority (Bradney 1985). The final condition clearly is not met. Ethnic and religious minorities continue to experience routine discrimination as a result of the deliberate efforts or the inadvertence of the state (Bradney 1993). When liberal commentators used the notion of free-speech to defend Salman Rushdie, writers from the ethnic and religious minorities responded with a charge of double-standards (Akhtar 1989; Sardar and Wyn Davies 1990). The same charge might be made if the parental right to object to sex education lessons was abolished.

Taking proper account of the needs of ethnic and religious minority groups cannot be accomplished in one area of law seen in isolation from other areas of law. If the law on sex education is going to attain a more satisfactory form than that found at present a more radical reappraisal of the relationship between political and legal structures on the one hand, and community needs and values on the other hand, is needed.

Notes

1. Scrutton J in *Re Carroll* [1931] 1 KB 317 at p.336; see also, Cross J in *Neville Estates Ltd v Madden* [1961] 3 All ER 769 at p.781.
2. National Curriculum Council (1990a), (1990b) and (1993).

6. Sex education and the law: working towards good practice

Rachel Thomson, Senior Development Officer, Sex Education Forum

The Sex Education Forum

The Sex Education Forum has worked since 1987 to develop a consensus among educators, health professionals, religious organisations and children's charities, supporting the entitlement of all young people to comprehensive and balanced sex education at school (Thomson and Scott 1992). The Forum has undertaken research into existing practice (*ibid.*), developed and disseminated models of good practice (Ray and Went 1995, Thomson 1993) and with other professional groups has sought clarification of the law and official guidance (legal opinions have been obtained from Williams 1993, Levy 1994, Beloff and Mountfield 1994). The professional consensus represented by the Sex Education Forum, that schools should provide young people with effective and appropriate sex education, is shared by the overwhelming majority of parents and young people (Allen 1987, NFER 1993). Yet, despite this support, the period since the inception of the Sex Education Forum has witnessed a politicisation of school sex education in the public and parliamentary spheres.

Many of the areas of sex education that are commonly conceived of as 'controversial' can and should be resolved by reference to principles of good practice. However, there continue to be a number of areas of legal uncertainty which require clarification and resolution. The chapters in this book outline these areas providing detailed legal commentaries. While the Sex Education Forum cannot formally associate itself with the opinions and conclusions set out in these chapters, it wishes to encourage informed debate in this area and to promote the best interest of the pupil and good practice in any interpretations or applications of the law to sex education in school. In this chapter I consider the main areas of sex education policy and practice that are currently contentious and, drawing on the Sex Education Forum's own guidance, suggest how schools may work within the present legislative framework to develop best practice and meet the needs of pupils (see also Sex Education Forum 1994).

The legislative context

School sex education did not receive any mention in primary legislation prior to the 1980s. Since that time it has been legislated on directly and indirectly four times (Education Act (No.2) 1986, Local Government Act 1988, Education Reform Act 1988, Education Act 1993). The causes of this politicisation are varied. The recent spate of legislation and controversy has been precipitated by a range of factors including the need for newspapers to maintain circulation; the increasing centralisation of educational policy, making it vulnerable to the lobbying of special interest groups; and a lack of consistency between different areas of government policy in education, health and social services. Unfortunately this close parliamentary attention has not always served to support schools, which have experienced almost ten years of permanent flux and many of which are still struggling to comply with legal requirements of eight years ago (Thomson and Scott 1992). Schools, having received little positive guidance or material support, are faced with a series of hurdles, which they must surmount in order to ensure pupils' entitlement.

Yet some of the legislative requirements have had positive effects. Despite the practical difficulties of the requirements of the Education (No.2) Act 1986, many schools have turned the legislative hurdles into opportunities, developing communication with the school community and outside agencies. Other legislation has been more damaging, in particular the rhetorical prohibitions of section 28 of the Local Government Act 1988 and the parental right of withdrawal from sex education (Education Act 1993; see the discussion in Chapter 1 by Neville Harris). The most negative impact has come from prohibitions on the content of sex education contained within Government guidance, for example warnings regarding the giving of contraceptive advice to pupils and the freedom of teachers to answer pupils' questions openly and honestly. In the absence of positive advice about the importance of this area of the curriculum, schools too often perceive sex education as a 'minefield', losing their own confidence as educators and their ability to exercise their own professional discretion in handling curriculum and classroom matters. The most common enquiries that the

Sex Education Forum receives from schools take the form of 'are we allowed to ...?'; rarely are we asked 'what is the best way to ...?'. Such a climate of uncertainty and confusion is not conducive to the development of confidence and good practice.

While it may be appropriate for primary legislation to define the general framework within which sex education should take place, the value of politicians and civil servants prescribing the content and delivery of the curriculum (which should meet the diverse needs of pupils) must be disputed. It is therefore important to distinguish between legal requirements set out in primary legislation, and guidance which is not legally binding. Most of the negative and often highly impractical prescriptions as to the way in which sex education should be provided are in the latter (DES 1987; DFE 1994). With the exception of the absolute right of parents to withdraw pupils from sex education, most people working in the field have no argument with the legal requirements on schools: to write a sex education policy; to deliver to all pupils sex education contained within the National Curriculum; to provide sex education to all secondary pupils which includes education about HIV/AIDS and sexually transmitted diseases (STDs) and to have regard to moral considerations and the value of family life. These legal requirements, with which schools are obliged to comply, are also requirements of good practice. The more detailed *advice* given in the Department for Education's guidance (DFE 1994) is not legally binding. It is the right of schools to take what they find useful from the guidance and, in consultation with their own community, to develop a framework for the delivery of sex education guided by their own needs and by principles of good practice.

Children's rights and parents' rights: the right of withdrawal

Andrew Bainham asks in his chapter 'just what happened to the rights of the child at school?' Despite advice from the Sex Education Forum and its member organisations, the policy makers and parliamentarians responsible for the 1993 Education Act did not take the interests of the child and pupil as their guiding focus. The establishment in law of an absolute right for parents to withdraw pupils from sex education, superseding the power of school governors to allow such withdrawal at their discretion, has created a significant contradiction between education legislation and other domestic and international law, as well as a practical minefield for schools. The only parallel for such a right in education is the right of parents to withdraw pupils from religious education.

Before this legislation was enacted, parents on occasion withdrew children from sex education. There has always been a small minority of parents, often from small religious groups such as the Plymouth Brethren, who have requested such action. Other larger religious and ethnic communities have generally been positive about school sex education, particularly where schools have taken steps to consult with them and to reflect religious and cultural diversity in the content and delivery of the programme. Where parents requested withdrawal in the past, after consultation and negotiation, most schools complied with such requests. By enshrining such practice in law, the Education Act 1993 has reframed the ethos of sex education from being guided by the needs of the pupil, to a situation where parental rights, and in some cases the fear of parental objection, have become the guiding force. The granting of a parental right of withdrawal from sex education has not solved any problems. However it has created some new difficulties for policy makers and schools. Most of these difficulties involve a conflict of interests between parents and pupils, which are more likely to arise in the area of sexuality than in any other area of the curriculum.

Before considering these difficulties it is necessary to be clear what the parental right of withdrawal actually is:

The parental right of withdrawal

- The parental right of withdrawal from sex education is absolute. Therefore if a parent is determined that their child should be withdrawn the request must be complied with. Parents are able to decide whether to withdraw pupils from all or parts of sex education.
- The right of withdrawal applies to parents of pupils, up to the age of 18, at maintained schools. It does not apply to the parents of young people at sixth form colleges or colleges of further education. It does apply to sixth form pupils in maintained schools.
- The right of withdrawal only covers those aspects of sex education that are not part of the National Curriculum. A child who has been withdrawn must still receive those aspects of sex education that are included in the science curriculum. Where sex education arises naturally as part of other National Curriculum subject areas such as English (including drama) or history, pupils should not be withdrawn.

If the school and the parents disagree

Technically parents do not have to provide any explanation of their reasons for withdrawing a pupil from sex education. However, parents who request withdrawal may not be well informed of the nature of the sex education programme and it is important that schools offer parents comprehensive information and reassurance. Research suggests that many parents do not feel adequately consulted in this area (NFER 1993). Some parents will be reassured about the content of the sex education programme after discussion and may allow the pupils to attend. Others may be prepared to allow the pupils to attend if single sex classes are provided for parts of the programme. Schools should take all possible steps to enable pupils to receive their entitlement in respect of sex education.

While there may be strong grounds for schools to demand that acceptable reasons for withdrawal are given, the Department for Education Circular notes that schools are only empowered to invite parents to discuss their concerns. Where the school has concerns about possible abuse, child protection procedures should be followed.

If the child and parent(s) disagree

Schools may be faced with a situation where a pupil has been withdrawn from sex education by their parents, yet wishes to attend the lesson(s). In such a situation the pupil does not have a right to this education against their parents' wishes, other than those aspects that are part of the science curriculum or arise naturally in other subject areas. In such a situation consultation with parents would be recommended together with the provision of books and leaflets for education at home.

A pupil has a right to challenge their parents' decision to withdraw them from sex education. This would involve applying to the courts (if under 16 with the support of a guardian *ad litem*) for a 'specific issue order' under sections 8 and 10 of the Children Act 1989. As Andrew Bainham notes in his chapter, this course of action is complicated and it is uncertain whether the courts would decide in favour of the child. Where the pupil is aged 16 or over there is a good chance of the court ruling in their favour. The success of such an independent application to the courts for a hearing would rely in part on the court's opinion of the maturity of the applicant, having implications for pupils with learning difficulties.

In practice, where a pupil and their parents disagree about withdrawal the best and most effective action for a school would be to encourage communication between parents and child. In many cases parents can be reassured by the school if they are convinced that the school has heard their concerns and is prepared to respond to them. Where a compromise is not possible a pupil would still be able to receive some formal education through science lessons and would have the right to information through the library, leaflets etc. Information could also be given as to other sources of education, for example, the school nurse, youth service, young people's health clinics (for example Brook Advisory Centres) and GPs.

If the parents disagree

It is possible that schools will face a situation where the pupil's parents disagree as to whether the pupil should be withdrawn from sex education. This is an issue that is not dealt with by the Department for Education's Circular, yet one that schools are already experiencing. In such a situation the parent who agrees with the child's wishes could apply to the court for a specific issue order under sections 8 and 10 of the Children Act 1989. Andrew Bainham suggests that in such a situation the courts would be more likely to intervene on the side of the child.

As other chapters note, there is a startling absence of children's rights in education. In its place a culture of parental rights has developed which is inconsistent with the development of parental responsibilities in other areas of the law. The concept of parental *responsibilities* assumes a 'contract' between parents and school that education is to be guided by the best interests of the child. In contrast the concept of parental rights assumes a basic antagonism between school and parent which overshadows the needs and integrity of the child. The absolute parental right of withdrawal is out of step with other domestic legislation and rulings such as the Children Act 1989 and the Gillick ruling. Nevertheless, while such a right (without conditions) is in statute, it is unlikely that the spirit of other statutes could be called upon to resolve disputes or uncertainties. It is more likely that international law will be called upon in order to assert children's rights in education, yet in order to access international law (which itself is ambiguous) domestic routes must first be exhausted.

Children's rights and parents' rights: contraceptive advice and confidentiality

Secondary school teachers will occasionally find themselves in situations where a pupil says 'Help, I think I might be pregnant, but my parents mustn't know'. In their response to this situation teachers need to ensure two things: first, that they do not refuse the pupil's request for help; and secondly, that they do not place themselves on the wrong side of the law.

The law in this area is inconclusive. There is no direct legislation that defines or prescribes a teacher's role. The most relevant legal precedent is that of *Gillick v West Norfolk and Wisbech Area Health Authority and another* (1986) which referred to a parent's challenge to the right of doctors to provide confidential contraceptive treatment to a girl under the age of 16 without parental consent. The majority judgment was that if conditions of maturity and understanding were fulfilled, doctors could treat such patients confidentially. The principles of *Gillick*, while having great relevance to educational settings, strictly only apply to medical settings and personnel. It is unfortunate that in developing guidance for schools, the Department for Education did not adapt the *Gillick* model, in order to (as Bridgeman puts it in Chapter 3) support 'teachers to exercise their professional judgement to act in the best interests of the individual pupil' and give guidance on 'the kind of factors which may be of relevance when deciding the content of the vague notion of best interests'. Such criteria would have helped teachers judge the risk faced by the pupil and would have helped to establish an explicit procedure that would have protected both themselves and pupils.

The only law directly relevant to the situation of a teacher considering whether to provide a pupil with confidential contraceptive advice, or whether to inform their parents of sexual activity below the age of consent, is the criminal law. To be breaking the law a teacher would have to be proved guilty of aiding and abetting a criminal offence. That is, it would have to be established that by providing a pupil with advice on contraception, or access to contraception, they had facilitated a crime (under age sex). Despite the provocative language of the Department for Education's Circular 5/94, legal opinion suggests that a teacher would only be in danger of committing such an offence if it could be proved, beyond reasonable doubt, that in their professional opinion they were *not* acting in the best interests of the child, and that they sought to facilitate the commission of a crime, *rather* than to avoid the unwanted consequences of sexual intercourse.

The advice that the Sex Education Forum and others have received from leading lawyers concurs with opinion expressed in other chapters of this book, that the Department for Education's guidance is 'alarmist' and does not provide an authoritative statement of the law. Below I will summarise the existing legal position, drawing on legal opinions received by the Forum and others, and consider how good practice would relate to this framework.

What a teacher is legally entitled to do

In her chapter, Jo Bridgeman notes that the Department for Education guidance (1994) 'seeks to use uncertainty to effect the particular moral stance which those devising the guidelines wished to reflect'. By introducing alarmist hints of criminality the guidance creates a very negative climate within which the needs and interests of pupils are marginalised. The effect of such guidance is to encourage caution and inaction and for teachers to be concerned with self protection at the expense of the protection and support of the pupil who is in urgent need of help. It may therefore be constructive to state what a teacher is legally entitled to do when approached for help from a pupil.

- A teacher is legally entitled to give any pupil information on sources of confidential contraceptive advice. Such advice may be sought from the school nurse, GP or young people's health clinic. A teacher is entitled to give the pupil information, leaflets etc., and even to make an appointment for them or to accompany them to the clinic.
- A teacher is not required by law to inform the pupil's parents of their request for help or contraceptive advice. It is a matter for their own professional discretion (taking account of the sex education policy of the school) as to whether they inform or involve any other parties. As Jo Bridgeman notes in Chapter 3, 'in practical terms, teachers should exercise their professional judgement and in appropriate cases maintain the confidences of pupils.'

Confidentiality

Again, the legal situation regarding confidentiality is far from clear. It is important that schools handle confidentiality issues in a way that is consistent and protects the interests of both pupils and staff. Schools should have an established procedure for dealing with confidentiality, which is understood by parents pupils and staff, rather than develop ad hoc arrangements in response to crises.

It is unlikely that the relationship between a pupil and a teacher is such that a legal duty of confidentiality would exist in the same form as it does between a doctor and a patient. However, a duty of confidentiality does exist between a young person and the school nurse or doctor, if it is in a one-to-one situation rather than a classroom setting. Health professionals, based in schools are able to offer confidential contraceptive advice and treatment to pupils.

Legal opinion suggests that a pupil does not have the right to demand confidentiality from a teacher. In turn, the teacher does not have a duty of confidentiality to the pupil but does have a power to break confidentiality (for example to inform parents or the head teacher) if, in their professional judgement, the pupil's interests are best served by doing so. Teachers should not promise confidentiality to pupils. Faced by a pupil requesting that information is kept secret a teacher should clearly state that they are prepared to help them, but without hearing the disclosure they cannot promise to keep it secret. It is a matter for the professional judgement of the teacher whether a confidence is maintained having heard the information.

The advice from the Department for Education and the Welsh Office does not place an absolute duty on teachers to break confidences, nor is there any legal requirement for teachers to inform parents of matters which a pupil has confided to them. Teachers are, however, bound by their contract of employment. If they are directly instructed by their employer, the head teacher and/or school governors to disclose the confidences of pupils, they could face disciplinary measures if they do not comply.

There are a number of practical steps that schools can take to minimise situations where confidences are broken:

- By using ground rules in sex education classes, which state clearly that personal experiences will not be shared within the classroom.
- By communicating clearly to pupils the limits of the teacher's role regarding confidentiality, and to inform pupils of other sources of help where confidentiality is assured, for example the school nurse, counsellor, GP or young people's health service (for example Brook Advisory Centres). Many young people are not aware that they can get confidential contraceptive advice from their GP or family planning services.
- By including confidentiality in the school sex education policy and communicating the school policy clearly to parents. The experience of most schools is that parents welcome schools providing pupils with confidential help if the young person feels unable at that point to confide in their parents.
- By always encouraging pupils to talk to their parents and by

actively supporting this dialogue both at the moment when help is sought and subsequently.

A procedure for judging risk

While *Gillick* applies only to health professionals, it has relevance to those working in educational settings. The Fraser guidelines (1985) (which formed part of *Gillick*) list factors which a doctor must consider prior to providing contraceptive advice and treatment to a young person under the age of 16 without parental advice. These guidelines could be adapted by schools in order to create a procedure for judging the degree to which a young person is at risk and the scope for granting confidentiality. The guidelines require doctors to satisfy themselves of the following:

- the young person will understand the doctor's advice
- the doctor cannot persuade the young person to inform his or her parents or allow the doctor to inform his or her parents that he or she is seeking contraceptive advice
- the young person is very likely to begin or to continue having intercourse with or without contraceptive treatment
- unless he or she receives contraceptive treatment, the young person's physical or mental health are likely to suffer
- the young person's best interests require the doctor to give contraceptive advice, treatment or both without parental consent.

Some of these conditions are not directly relevant to an educational setting, but others are, for example: encouraging the young person to talk to their parents; acknowledging the physical and mental risks of pregnancy; and a consideration of the pupil's best interests. Faced with disclosure from a pupil of pregnancy, a school will have some additional considerations. A school should be concerned if the sex education that they have provided has not served to educate the young person adequately. They may therefore wish to review the timing of their sex education, or to ensure that information be made available to pupils as to where confidential advice and treatment may be obtained. A school may also wish to establish the young person is not at risk of sexual abuse. Their child protection procedures should be invoked if they perceive such a risk. The following extract from a secondary school sex education policy outlines the way in which a school may decide to handle issues of contraceptive advice and confidentiality:

> Pupils will be made aware that some information cannot be held confidential, and made to understand that if certain disclosures are made

certain actions will ensue. At the same time pupils will be offered sensitive and appropriate support. The following procedure will be adhered to by all adults.

- Disclosure or suspicion of possible abuse – the school's child protection policy will be invoked.
- Disclosure of pregnancy or advice on contraception – it is hoped that the following procedure will ensure that pupils who are in difficulty know that they can talk to an adult in the school and that they will be supported.
- Professional information and guidance will always be sought from a health professional.
- The school will always encourage pupils to talk with their parents first:
  – pupils should be asked whether they can tell their parent(s) and whether they want help in doing so. If this takes place subsequent responsibility lies with the parent(s). It will need to be checked;
  – if pupils refuse to tell their parent(s) the adult should refer them to a health professional;
  – the adult should report the incident to the head teacher who will consult with the health professional about informing the parent(s). (Sex Education Forum 1994)

It is easy to underestimate the significance of confidentiality for young people. The primary concerns of a young person who might disclose information to a teacher are that their trust is respected and that help is forthcoming. It is vital that teachers do not betray a young person's trust and that they ensure that their request for help is honoured. Many young people find it extremely difficult to trust adults, be they doctors, parents or teachers. If their trust is betrayed they may refuse to seek help in the future. Young people are unlikely to be conscious of the possible legal consequences of such disclosures and it is important that schools create an environment in which staff have sufficient confidence to be guided by the best interests of the pupil rather than by fear of the law. A well thought out and disseminated policy on confidentiality and a comprehensive sex education programme where pupils are educated about their rights to confidentiality from different professional groups, and where they can go for help, should help to minimise such disclosures. Where such disclosures do arise, schools should be prepared in advance. Further detailed guidance on developing good practice in this area is available from Brook Advisory Centres (White 1995).

Lesbian and gay issues

It is important to remember that there may be lesbian or gay pupils who are sexually active and who might need or request sexual health advice. While the legal age of consent for gay men is now 18, there is no legal age of consent for lesbians. Faced by a request for help by a young man below the age of 18 who may disclose that he is involved in a sexual relationship with a man, a school should follow the guidance given above regarding confidentiality.

Even though they are in a minority, a significant proportion of young people are or will become lesbian or gay. Many young people come from families which include lesbians or gay men, and all young people will live in a society with a diversity of sexual lifestyles and identities. It is important that schools do not ignore this in the education that they provide. Section 28 of the local Government Act 1988 applies to the activities of local authorities and not to schools. There is no prohibition on schools including lesbian and gay issues and perspectives in their sex education programmes. Unfortunately many schools are very nervous about this area and many continue to believe, mistakenly, that they are not allowed to teach about homosexuality. A recent survey with young people found that it was the area that they most wanted to learn more about yet the one on which they received least education (Rudyat and others 1992). Other research carried out with lesbians and gay men found that they experienced a great deal of bullying at school and received little, if any, education which they felt was relevant to them or supportive of them (Stonewall 1994).

Conclusion

Schools have to work within the existing legislative framework and the Sex Education Forum works to support them in this task. The Sex Education Forum is not convinced that the parental right of withdrawal was either necessary or desirable, and works with schools and professionals to minimise its exercise and to maximise the entitlement of pupils to sex education at school. The increasing emphasis on parental rights in education places new demands on schools to develop communication and partnership with pupils' families. For many schools this is unfamiliar territory and a task for which they will require support and encouragement. The Forum is currently working to develop guidance for schools on partnership with parents with the aim of minimising the exercise of parental withdrawal from sex education. Nevertheless the Sex Education Forum's focus continues to be on the quality of the sex education received by pupils themselves. If the quality and environment within which sex education is delivered can be strengthened by closer consultation with parents, families and the broader community, all parties will benefit, particularly (and most importantly) the pupils themselves. Work undertaken by the Sex Education Forum suggests that partnership with parents has an extremely positive impact. This is particularly the case where there are a high proportion of pupils from minority ethnic groups, whose experiences may not be understood by the teaching staff or reflected in the sex education resources used.

Where the law is unclear professional guidance has great weight. The Sex Education Forum is working with its members and other professional bodies such as teaching unions, in order to develop a positive consensus as to good practice. The aim of this work is to give teachers and other professional groups the confidence to work in a way that prioritises the best interests of the young person. In the area of confidentiality and contraceptive advice the development of a positive professional consensus is an urgent priority. Concerns over confidentiality and potential criminal liability for teachers are also emerging in the area of drugs education in schools, giving further weight to the need for a clear statement of the best interests of the child within the educational context. Any future policy development in this area will need to be based on a pragmatic acceptance of the reality of young people's behaviour. That this behaviour may not always be legal should not prevent young people from seeking and receiving help and support. Policy should also be guided by the best interests of the child or young person and a positive understanding of prevention and risk reduction.

Given the strain caused by the weight of legislation in this area in the last decade the Sex Education Forum is cautious about calling for further changes to the law or the curriculum. However, the Forum sees the following as providing an enduring framework for this area of the curriculum:

- sex education to become part of the National Curriculum, thus securing the entitlement of pupils
- a requirement for school governors to develop a written sex education policy in consultation with parents and the wider community, including a values statement, and for the policy to be regularly reviewed and the programme regularly evaluated to ensure that the needs of all pupils are met
- for the Department for Education and Employment to issue guidance to schools on confidentiality and contraceptive

advice, confirming the exercise of the professional discretion of teachers and suggesting factors for determining the pupil's best interests

- for health professionals to provide school based confidential counselling services for pupils, possibly in the form of school based health clinics.

Appendix I

Extracts from relevant statutes, instruments and official guidance

A. U.K. legislation

Children and Young Persons Act 1933

1. Cruelty to persons under 16

(1) If any person who has attained the age of 16 years and has the custody, charge, or care of any child or young person under that age, wilfully assaults, ill-treats, neglects, abandons, or exposes him, or causes or procures him to be assaulted, ill-treated, neglected, abandoned, or exposed, in manner likely to cause him unnecessary suffering or injury to health ..., that person shall be guilty of [an offence] ...

(2) For the purposes of this section –

(a) A parent or other person legally liable to maintain a child or young person shall be deemed to have neglected him in a manner likely to cause injury to his health if he has failed to provide adequate food, clothing, medical aid or lodging for him, or if, having been unable otherwise to provide such food, clothing, medical aid or lodging, he has failed to take steps to procure it to be provided under [the enactments applicable in that behalf].

Education Act 1944

36. Duty of parents to secure the education of their children

It shall be the duty of the parent of every child of compulsory school age to cause him to receive efficient full-time education suitable to his age, ability, and aptitude, and to any special educational needs he may have or by regular attendance at school or otherwise.

76. Pupils to be educated in accordance with the wishes of their parents

In the exercise and performance of all powers and duties conferred and imposed on them by the Education Acts 1944 to 1993 the Secretary of State for Education, the funding authorities and local education authorities shall have regard to the general principle that, so far as is compatible with the provision of efficient construction and training and the avoidance of unreasonable public expenditure, pupils are to be educated in accordance with the wishes of their parents.

114. Interpretation

(1) In this Act, unless the context otherwise requires, the following expressions have the meanings hereby respectively assigned to them, that is to say:

'Sex Education' includes education about –

(a) Acquired Immune Deficiency Syndrome and Human Immuno-deficiency Virus and

(b) any other sexually transmitted disease ...

'Young person' means a person of compulsory school age who has not attained the age of 18 years.

(1D) In this Act, unless context otherwise requires, 'parent' in relation to a child or young person, includes any person –

(a) who is not a parent of his but has parental responsibility for him, or

(b) who has care of him,

except for the purposes of the enactments mentioned in sub-section (1E) of this section, where it only includes such a person if he is an individual.

The Sexual Offences Act 1956

5. Intercourse with a girl under thirteen

It is a felony for a man to have unlawful sexual intercourse with a girl under the age of thirteen.

6. Intercourse with a girl between thirteen and sixteen

(1) It is an offence, subject to the exceptions mentioned in this section, for a man to have unlawful sexual intercourse with a girl ... under the age of sixteen ...

(3) A man is not guilty of an offence under this section because he has unlawful sexual intercourse with a girl under the age of sixteen, if he is under the age of twenty-four and has not previously been charged with a like offence, and he believes her to be of the age of sixteen or over and has reasonable cause for the belief …

28. Causing or encouraging prostitution of, intercourse with, or indecent assault on, a girl under sixteen

(1) It is an offence for a person to cause or encourage the prostitution of, or the commission of unlawful sexual intercourse with, or an indecent assault on, a girl under the age of sixteen for whom he is responsible.
(2) Where a girl has become a prostitute, or has had unlawful sexual intercourse, or has been indecently assaulted, a person shall be deemed for the purposes under this section to have caused or encouraged it, if he knowingly allowed her to consort with, or to enter or continue in the employment of, any prostitute or person of known immoral character.
(3) The persons who are to be treated under this section as responsible for a girl are (subject to sub section (4) of this section) –

   (a) her parents;
   (b) any person who is not a parent of hers but has parental responsibility for her;
   (c) any person who has care of her.

(4) An individual falling within sub section (3)(a) or (b) of this section is not to be treated as responsible for a girl if –

   (a) a residence order under the Children Act 1989 is in force with respect to her and he is not named in the order as the person with whom she is to live; or
   (b) a care order under that Act is in force with respect to her.

Family Law Reform Act 1969

8. Consent by persons under the age of sixteen to surgical, medical and dental treatment

(1) The consent of a minor who has attained the age of sixteen years to any surgical, medical or dental treatment which in the absence of consent, would constitute to a trespass to his person, shall be as effective as it would be if he were of full age; and where a minor has by virtue of this section given an effec-

tive consent to any treatment it shall not be necessary to obtain it from his parent or guardian.

(2) In this section "surgical, medical or dental treatment" includes any procedure undertaken for the purposes of diagnosis, and this section applies to any procedure (including, in particular, the administration of an anaesthetic) which is ancillary to that treatment as it applies to that treatment.

(3) Nothing in this section shall be construed as making ineffective any consent which would have been effective if this section had not been enacted.

National Health Service Act 1977

5. Other services

(1) It is the Secretary of State's duty –

...

(b) to arrange, to such extent as he considers necessary to meet all reasonable requirements in England and Wales, for the giving on advice of contraception, the medical examination of persons seeking advice on contraception, the treatment of such persons and the supply of contraceptive substances and appliances.

Education No.2 Act 1986

18. County, controlled and maintained special schools

(1) The articles of government for every county, controlled and special school shall provide for it to be the duty of the governing body to consider –

(a) the policy of the local education authority as to the secular curriculum for the authority's schools, as expressed in the statement made by the authority under section 17 of this Act;

(b) what, in their opinion, should be the aims of the secular curriculum for the school; and

(c) how (if at all) the authority's policy with regard to matters other than sex education should in their opinion be modified in relation to the school;

and to make and keep up to date a written statement of their conclusions.

(2) The articles of government for every such school shall provide for it to be the duty of the governing body –

(a) to consider separately (while having regard to the local education authority's statement under section 17 of this Act) the question whether sex education should form part of the secular curriculum for the school:

(b) to make, and keep up to date, a separate written statement –

(i) of their policy with regard to the content and organisation of the relevant part of the curriculum; or

(ii) where they conclude that sex education should form part of the secular curriculum, of that conclusion.*

* *Note: Sub section (2) must be read in conjunction with s.241(6) of the Education Act 1993 (below), which excludes from its scope secondary schools and secondary-age pupils in special schools.*

(3) The articles of government for every such school shall provide for it to be the duty of the governing body –

(a) when considering the matters mentioned in sub sections (1) and (2) above, to do so in consultation with the head teacher and to have regard –

(i) to any representations which are made to them, with regard to any of those matters, by any person connected to the community served by that school;

(ii) to any such representations which are made to them by the Chief officer of police and which are connected with his responsibilities;

(b) to consult the authorities before making or varying any statement under sub section (1) above ...

46. Sex education

The local education authority by whom any county, voluntary or special school is maintained, and the governing body or head teacher of the school, shall take such steps as are reasonably practicable to secure that where sex education is given to any registered pupils at a school it is given in such a manner as to encourage those pupils to have due regard to moral considerations and the value of family life.

46A. Application of sections 44 to 46 to grant-maintained schools

Sections 44 to 46 of this Act shall apply in relation to the governing body and head teacher of, and the junior pupils and other pupils at, a grant-maintained school as they apply in relation to the governing body and head teacher of, and the junior pupils and other pupils at, a county, voluntary or maintained special school.

Education Reform Act 1988

1. Duties with respect to the curriculum

...

(2) The curriculum for a maintained school satisfies the requirements of this section if it is a broadly based curriculum which –

(a) promotes the spiritual, moral, cultural, mental and physical development of pupils of the school and of society; and
(b) prepares such pupils for the opportunities, responsibilities and experiences of adult life.

2. The National Curriculum

(1) The curriculum for every maintained school shall comprise a basic curriculum which includes -

(a) provision for religious education for all registered pupils of the school;
(aa) in the case of a secondary school, provision for sex education for all registered pupils at the school;
(ab) in the case of a special school, provision for sex education for all registered pupils at the school who are provided with secondary education; and
(b) a curriculum for all registered pupils at the school of compulsory school age (to be known as 'the National Curriculum') which meets the requirements of sub section (2).

9. Exceptions, special arrangements and supplementary and consequential provisions

...

(3) If the parent of any pupil in attendance at any maintained school requests that he may be wholly or partly excused -

(a) from attendance at religious worship in the school;
(b) from receiving religious education given in the school in accordance with the school's basic curriculum; or
(c) both from such attendance and from receiving such education;

the pupil shall be so excused accordingly until the request is withdrawn.

17A. Exemption from sex education

[see Education Act 1993, section 241 below]

23. Complaints and enforcement

(1) Every local education authority shall, with the approval of the Secretary of State and after consultation with governing bodies of aided schools and special agreement schools, make arrangements for the consideration and disposal of any complaint made on or after the 1st September 1989 which is to the effect that the authority, or the governing body of any county or voluntary school maintained by the authority or any special school so maintained which is not established in a hospital –

(a) have acted or are proposing to act unreasonably with respect to the exercise or any power conferred or the performance of any duty imposed on them by or under –

(i) any provision of this Chapter; or

(ii) any other enactment relating to the curriculum for, or religious worship, in maintained schools other than grant-maintained schools; or

(b) have failed to discharge any such duty.

(2) The Secretary of State shall not entertain under section 68 or 99 of the 1944 Act any complaint falling within sub section (1) above, unless a complaint concerning the same matter has been made and disposed of in accordance with arrangements made under that sub section.

Local Government Act 1988

28. Prohibition on promoting homosexuality by teaching or by publishing material

(1) The following section shall be inserted after section 2 of the Local Government Act 1986 (prohibition of political publicity) –

"2A(1) a local authority shall not –

(a) intentionally promote homosexuality or publish material with the intention of promoting homosexuality;

(b) promote the teaching in any maintained school of the

acceptability of homosexuality as a pretended family relationship.

(2) Nothing in sub section 1 shall be taken to prohibit the doing of anything for the purpose of preventing the spread of disease …"

Education Act 1993

161. Duties of the governing body etc. in relation to pupils with special educational needs

…

(4) Where a child who has special educational needs, is being educated in a county, voluntary or grant-maintained school or a maintained nursery school, those concerned with making special educational provision for the child shall secure, so far as is reasonably practicable and is compatible with -

(a) the child receiving the special educational provision which his learning difficulty calls for,
(b) the provision of efficient education for the children with whom he will be educated, and
(c) the efficient use of resources,

that the child engages in the activities of the school together with children who do not have special educational needs.

188. Approval of special schools

…

(6) Regulations shall make provision for securing that, so far as practicable, every pupil attending a special school –

(a) receives religious education and attends religious worship, or
(b) is withdrawn from receiving such education or from attendance at such worship in accordance with the wishes of his parent.

241. Sex education

(1) In section 2(1) of the Education Reform Act 1988 (content of curriculum), after "school" in paragraph (a) there is inserted –

"(aa) in the case of a secondary school, provision for sex education for all registered pupils at the school;
(ab) in the case of a special school, provision for education for

all registered pupils at the school who are provided with secondary education".

(2) In section 114(1) of the Education Act 1944 (interpretation), after the definition of "Senior pupil" there is inserted –

'Sex education' includes education about –

(a) Acquired Immune Deficiency Syndrome and Human Immunodeficiency Virus, and
(b) any other sexually transmitted disease".

(3) After section 17 of the Education Reform Act 1988 there is inserted –

"*Exemption from sex education*

17A. If the parent of any pupil in attendance at any maintained school requests that he may be wholly or partly excused from receiving sex education at the school, the pupil shall, except so far as such education is comprised in the National Curriculum, be so excused accordingly until the request is withdrawn".

(4) The Secretary of State shall so exercise the power conferred by section 4 of that Act to revise the National Curriculum as to secure that the subject of science does not include –

(a) Acquired Immune Deficiency Syndrome and Human Immuno-deficiency Virus,
(b) any other sexually transmitted disease, or
(c) aspects of human sexual behaviour, other than biological aspects,

and sections 20, 21 and 232(4) of that Act (procedure for making orders) and section 242 of this Act, shall not apply to any order made only for the purposes of this sub section.

(5) The governing body of every maintained or grant-maintained school, and, in relation to pupils who are provided with secondary education, the governing body of every maintained special school shall –

(a) make, and keep up to date, a separate written statement of their policy with regard to the provision of sex education, and
(b) make copies of the statement available for inspection (at all reasonable times) by parents of registered pupils at the school and provide a copy of the statement free of charge to any such parent who asks for one.

(6) In relation to any county, or controlled, secondary school, and in relation to any pupils who are provided with secondary edu-

cation in a maintained special school, section 18 of the Education (No.2) Act 1986 (policy for curriculum in county etc. schools), shall have effect with the omission of sub sections (2) and (6)(c)(i) and of the references to the matters mentioned in sub section (2) of that section.

Criminal Justice and Public Order Act 1994

143. Male rape and buggery

(1) Section 12 of the Sexual Offences Act 1956 (offence of buggery) shall be amended as follows:
(2) In sub section (1), after the words "another person" there shall be inserted the words "otherwise than in the circumstances described in sub section (1A) below".
(3) After sub section (1), there shall be inserted the following sub sections

"(1A)The circumstances referred to in sub section (1) are that the act of buggery takes place in private and that both parties have attained the age of eighteen.

(1B) An act of buggery of one man with another shall not be treated as taking place in private if it takes place -

(a) when more than two persons take part or are present

...

(1C) in any proceedings of a person for buggery with another person it shall be for the prosecutor to prove that the act of buggery took place otherwise than in private or that one of the parties to it had not attained the age of eighteen".

B. International treaties

European Convention on Human Rights 1950

First protocol, Article 2

No person shall be denied the right to education. In the exercise of any functions which it assumes in relation to education and to teaching, the State shall respect the right of parents to ensure such education and teaching in conformity with their own religious and philosophical convictions.

UN Convention on the Rights of the Child 1989

Article 28 — Education

1. State Parties recognize the right of the child to education, and with view to achieving this right progressively and on the basis of equal opportunity, they shall, in particular:
   a) make primary education compulsory and available to all;
   b) encourage the development of different forms of secondary education, including general and vocational education, make them available and accessible to every child, and take appropriate measures such as the introduction of free education and offering financial assistance in case of need;
   c) make higher education accessible to all on the basis of capacity by every appropriate means;
   d) make educational and vocational information and guidance available and accessible to all children;
   e) take measures to encourage regular attendance at schools and the reduction of drop-out rates.

The Child's right to education, and the State's duty to ensure that primary education at least is made free and compulsory. Administration of school discipline is to reflect the child's human dignity. Emphasis is laid on the need for international co-operation to ensure this right.

2. States Parties shall take all appropriate measures to ensure that school discipline is administered in a manner consistent with the child's human dignity and in conformity with the present Convention.
3. States Parties shall promote and encourage international co-operation in matters relating to education, in particular with a view to contributing to the elimination of ignorance and illiteracy throughout the world and facilitating access to scientific and technical knowledge and modern teaching methods. In this regard, particular account shall be taken of the needs of developing countries.

Article 29

1. States Parties agree that the education of the child shall be directed to:
   a) the development of the child's personality, talents and mental and physical abilities to their potential;
   b) the development of respect for human rights and fundamental freedoms, and for the principles enshrined in the Charter of the United Nations;

Education

The State's recognition that the eduction should be directed at developing the child's personality and talents, preparing the child for active life as an adult, fostering respect for basic fullest human rights and developing respect for the child's own cultural and national values and those of others.

c) the development of respect for the child's parents, his or her own cultural identity, language and values, for the national values of the country in which the child is living, the country from which he or she may originate, and for civilisations different from his or her own;
d) the preparation of the child for responsible life in a free society, in the spirit of understanding, peace, tolerance, equality of sexes, and friendship among all peoples, ethnic, national and religious groups and persons of indigenous origin;
e) the development of respect for the natural environment.

2. No part of this article or article 28 shall be constructed so as to interfere with the Liberty of individuals and bodies to establish and direct education institutions, subject always to the observance of the principles set forth in paragraph 1 of this article and to the requirements that the education given in such institutions shall conform to such minimum standards as may be laid down by the State.

C. Department for Education guidance on sex education

Education Act 1993: Sex education in schools – Circular 5/94 (extracts)

The role of parents

7. The prime responsibility for bringing up children rests with parents. Schools should therefore recognise that parents are key figures in helping their children to cope with the emotional and physical aspects of growing up and in preparing them for the challenges and responsibilities which sexual maturity brings. The teaching offered by schools should be complementary and supportive to the role of parents, and should have regard to parents' views about its content and presentation. The more successful schools are in achieving this, the less the likelihood that parents will wish to exercise their right of withdrawal.

8. The Secretary of State recognises that sex education is a difficult issue which will place demands on schools and teachers. But it is an important part of children's preparation for adult life, and he is very grateful to teachers for the contribution they make to this. In his view, the purpose of sex education should be to provide knowledge about loving relationships, the nature of sexuality and the processes of human reproduction. At the same time it should lead to the acquisition of understanding and attitudes which prepare pupils to view their relationships in a responsible and healthy

manner. It must not be value-free; it should also be tailored not only to the age but also to the understanding of pupils. The Secretary of State believes that schools' programmes of sex education should therefore aim to present facts in an objective, balanced and sensitive manner, set within a clear framework of values and an awareness of the law on sexual behaviour. Pupils should accordingly be encouraged to appreciate the value of stable family life, marriage and the responsibilities of parenthood. They should be helped to consider the importance of self-restraint, dignity, respect for themselves and others, acceptance of responsibility, sensitivity towards the needs and views of others, loyalty and fidelity. And they should be enabled to recognise the physical, emotional and moral implications, and risks, of certain types of behaviour, and to accept that both sexes must behave responsibly in sexual matters. Teachers need to acknowledge that many children come from backgrounds that do not reflect such values or experiences. Sensitivity is therefore needed to avoid causing hurt and offence to them and their families: and to allow such children to feel a sense of worth. But teachers should also help pupils, whatever their circumstances, to raise their sights.

The context of sex education

9. In July 1992 the Government published its health strategy in the White Paper "The Health of the Nation" which identifies sexual health as one of the five key areas in which substantial improvement in health could be achieved. The White Paper set a number of relevant objectives and targets, including a reduction in the rate of conceptions among the under-16s by 50 per cent by the year 2000, and lessening the incidence of HIV, AIDS and other sexually transmitted diseases. Education has a vital part to play in achieving these and other Health of the Nation targets: sex education, given within the framework described above, can make a substantial contribution.

10. In **primary schools**, the Secretary of State considers that very great care should be taken to match any sex education provided to the maturity of the pupils involved, which may not always correspond to their chronological age. It should take account both of their capacity to absorb sensitive information and of the extent to which it is essential for them to have such information at that point in their development. This should be geared to the needs of the class or group as a whole, and should not be determined by the pace of the most precocious pupils whose needs can be met in other

ways (see paragraph 31 below). At the primary stage, the aim should be to prepare pupils to cope with the physical and emotional challenges of growing up, and to give them an elementary understanding of human reproduction. Pupils' questions should be answered sensitively: due consideration should be given to any particular religious or cultural factors bearing on the discussion of sexual issues, and to parents' wishes as to the degree of explicitness of the concepts and presentation to be used. Handling of these matters will place demands on teachers' professional skills, which the Secretary of State is confident they will be able to meet.

11. The law does not define the purpose and content of sex education, other than declaring that it includes education about HIV and AIDS and other sexually transmitted diseases. In **secondary schools** sex education should, in the Secretary of State's view, encompass, in addition to facts about human reproductive processes and behaviour, consideration of the broader emotional and ethical dimensions of sexual attitudes. It must include, at a point appropriate to the age and maturity of the pupils, education about HIV and AIDS and other sexually transmitted diseases. In dealing with these and other sensitive matters, such as contraception and abortion, schools should aim to offer balanced and factual information and to acknowledge the major moral and ethical issues involved. Where schools are founded on specific religious principles, this may have a direct bearing on the manner in which such subjects are presented. The considerations set out in paragraph 10 above will also be relevant at the secondary stage.

12. **Special schools** have a particularly sensitive role to play. Children with learning difficulties are entitled to the same opportunity as other children to benefit from sex education. They may need more help than others in coping with the physical and emotional aspects of growing up; they may also need more help in learning what sorts of behaviour are and are not acceptable, and in being warned and prepared against unacceptable behaviour by adults. Schools should bear in mind that some parents of children with special educational needs may find it difficult to come to terms with the idea that their children will some day become sexually active.

13. (Omitted)

The role of governors in primary schools

14. Governing bodies of **county, controlled and grant-main-**

tained primary schools (including middle schools deemed primary) have the duty to decide:

a. whether their school should provide sex education, and if so
b. what it should consist of, and how it should be organised.

15. Governing bodies of **voluntary aided and special agreement primary schools** are not obliged to comply with these detailed requirements, but will need to consider the question of provision of sex education as part of their wider responsibilities relating to the curriculum offered by their school. The Secretary of State hopes that they will voluntarily adopt similar arrangements to those applying at other maintained primary schools. Furthermore, they will be subject to the requirement in section 241(5) of the Education Act 1993, which applies to the governing bodies of **all maintained primary and secondary schools** (except special schools – see paragraph 26 and Annex A), to have a written statement of whatever policy they adopt on sex education and to make it available to parents on request.

16. In developing their policies, governing bodies will wish to bear in mind that certain elements of the National Curriculum Science Order are relevant. The Secretary of State will this summer make an Order as required by section 241(4) of the Education Act 1993. The effect of this Order will be to prohibit the teaching, **as part of the National Curriculum in Science**, of any material on AIDS, HIV, and other sexually transmitted diseases, or any aspect, other than biological aspects, of human sexual behaviour. Accordingly, with effect from September 1994 these topics will not form part of the National Curriculum.

17. There are likely to be further changes to the Science Order from September 1995, following consultation this summer about the revision of the subject Orders generally in the light of Sir Ron Dearing's review of the National Curriculum. However, subject to the outcome of that consultation, the Secretary of State intends that there should continue to be a requirement for pupils at Key Stages 1 and 2 to be taught about human development and reproduction. As for all topics which are specified in the National Curriculum, parents are not entitled to withdraw their children from this teaching.

18. In discharging their duties relating to sex education, governors must take such steps as are reasonably practicable to ensure that any provision they make accords with the requirement of

section 46 of the Education (No.2) Act 1986 that it should encourage pupils to have due regard to moral considerations and the value of family life. They are also required to have regard to any representations made to them by anyone connected with the community served by the school. Governors may wish to take due account of representations or advice they may receive from health authorities and from others, in particular religious groups and ethnic minority communities. In the case of **county and controlled schools** the governors are statutorily required to consult the head.

19. The Secretary of State expects that governors will draw upon help and guidance from a number of sources. These might include the professional advice which the head and other school staff are able to offer; support and guidance from LEA advisory staff; the experience and expertise of individual members of the governing body; and the views of health authorities, including the school health service, school doctors and nurses. Governors may also find it helpful to take account of the references to sex education in the National Curriculum Council publication "Curriculum guidance 5: Health Education" (NCC, 1990); to family life education in "Curriculum guidance 8: Education for Citizenship" (NCC, 1990); and to moral considerations in the NCC discussion paper "Spiritual and Moral Development" (NCC, 1993).

20. The Secretary of State envisages that governors, as part of their responsibility for deciding policy on the **content** of any sex education to be offered, will determine their school's overall approach to teaching about sexual matters. In considering the school's choice of teaching materials from the wide range available, they should satisfy themselves that those selected are of high quality, are appropriate to the needs and ages of pupils, and conform with the overall requirements of section 46 of the 1986 Act relating to moral considerations and the value of family life. Governors should also determine how parents are to be consulted and informed, and what opportunities they might have to see teaching materials, and to receive explanations of the way in which it is proposed to use them in the classroom. A number of bodies maintain lists of available materials. Governors should also have a policy – informed by consultation with parents – on whether and how to use outside speakers on particular topics. That policy should include the steps to be taken by the governors or by the head teacher and staff to ensure that any contributions by such speakers are consistent with the governors' overall policy, with

statutory requirements and with good educational practice. It should cover the degree of explicitness of content and presentation, and arrangements for the presence or intervention of teachers as appropriate. Finally, the policy should refer to the **organisation** of sex education, and to the arrangements to be adopted to give effect to parents' right to withdraw their children from all or part of any sex education provided (see paragraphs 36-37). But in all these matters the governors should maintain the exercise by the head teacher and staff of their own professional skills in delivering the curriculum in accordance with that policy.

The role of governors in secondary schools

21. The governing bodies of **all secondary schools** (including middle schools deemed secondary) are required to ensure that their schools offer, for all registered pupils (including those over compulsory school age), a programme of sex education including education about HIV and AIDS and other sexually transmitted diseases. They must maintain a written statement of their policy on the provision of sex education, copies of which must be made available to parents on request.

24. All secondary schools must ensure that their curriculum deals with the topics specified in the Science Order. Again, it is for the governors to decide on its **organisation** in relation to other aspects of sex education. This will often be more complex than in primary schools. Secondary schools may, for example, deal with all sex education, including the elements outlined above, as a discrete topic; or within broader programmes of personal and social education; or within science education; or they may choose to satisfy the requirements of the Science Order within their teaching of biology, and to deal with wider aspects of sex education in separate lessons.

25. In deciding this, schools will need to take account of the fact that parents have a right to withdraw their children from any or all aspects of sex education (see paragraphs 36-37). In developing a policy on the **organisation** of the teaching of particular topics, governing bodies should therefore seek the advice of the head and other teaching staff so as to ensure that where children are withdrawn, there is no disruption to other elements of their education.

The role of governors in special schools

26. In those **special schools** which cater exclusively for pupils provided with secondary education, the responsibilities of governing bodies correspond to those of primary or secondary school gov-

erning bodies respectively, as outlined above. In special schools providing both primary and secondary education, the governing bodies need to adopt separate arrangements for children receiving education in those respective categories, corresponding to those applying to primary schools in the former case and to secondary schools in the latter. In any school, the arrangements adopted will need to take account of any modification of provision entailed by individual pupils' statements of special educational need.

The general role of governors in all maintained schools

27. **All maintained schools** must publish in their prospectus a summary of the content and organisation of any sex education they do provide. These should include an explanation of how parents who wish to discuss this issue can do so, and information about the means of putting into effect parents' right of withdrawal.

28. Many parents may find this information adequate. The Secretary of State hopes, however, that governing bodies will involve all parents as fully as possible in the formulation and review of their policies and programmes in this important area, both as a matter of good practice and because such involvement is likely to reduce the number of parents who have sufficiently strong reservations about the schools' programme as to lead them to consider exercising their right of withdrawal. Governing bodies already include some parents. Possible means of bringing all parents into the process include placing the topic in the annual report and on the agenda of the annual governors' meeting for parents, or holding specific meetings at which they are invited to contribute to the review or development of policy and practice on this issue. Particular attention should be paid to the needs of parents from some religious groups and ethnic minority communities who may not be comfortable in dealing with the subject publicly.

The role of the head and other teachers

29. The head and other teachers have an important part to play in contributing to the preparation, review and updating of the governing body's policy on sex education. They will also need to develop suitable procedures for dealing with parental requests for withdrawal, and to decide the alternative arrangements to be made for the supervision or teaching of any pupils whose parents exercise that right.

30. In advising governors on the content and organisation of sex education, the head and teaching staff should give particular

attention to the treatment of issues relating to sex education in different areas of the curriculum. It is inevitable, particularly in secondary schools, that the teaching of apparently unrelated topics will occasionally lead to a discussion of aspects of sexual behaviour. Provided that such discussion is relatively limited and set within the context of the other subject concerned, it will not necessarily constitute part of a programme of sex education for the purposes of the provisions set out in **Annex A**. In such cases, particularly where they involve pupils whose parents have withdrawn them from sex education as such, teachers will need to balance the need to give proper attention to relevant issues with the need to respect pupils' and parents' views and sensitivities. The Secretary of State is confident that teachers will draw upon their professional judgement and common sense to deal effectively with such occurrences. To forestall possible misunderstandings, it may well be helpful to ensure that this issue is covered in the school's written sex education policy.

31. There will be occasions when teachers and other professionals giving sex education have to exercise their discretion and judgement about how to deal with particularly explicit issues raised by an individual pupil. It is unlikely to be appropriate to deal with such issues with the whole class. Teachers should normally discuss the child's concerns first with the parents, to see how they would like the matter to be handled. Where the parents wish them to do so, it may be appropriate to respond individually to the child's question outside the class. In exceptional circumstances, where the teacher has reason to believe that a child may be distressed or in danger, it may be appropriate for the teacher to speak individually to the child, before consulting the parents, to clarify the basis for the concerns. Where there is a risk that a teacher might be compromised in these circumstances, it would be wise for them to be accompanied by another member of staff.

32. In implementing their school's policy on sex education, teachers should take account of the range of expertise and other resources available to them, including the contribution which health authorities, other health service bodies, and health professionals – particularly doctors (including GPs) and school nurses – may be able to make.

The role of the LEA

33. Section 17 of the 1986 Act requires LEAs to determine and state their policies in respect of the secular curriculum for **county,**

controlled and maintained special schools in their area, having considered the range and internal balance of that curriculum. In carrying out that duty, LEAs must have regard to the curriculum responsibilities laid upon them by section 1 of the 1988 Act. Any LEA policy statement which refers to sex education is subject to section 46 of the 1986 Act.

34. The LEA is required, under section 23 of the Education Reform Act 1988, to deal with complaints from parents of pupils at any county, voluntary or maintained special school in its area about that school's discharge of its responsibilities relating to the curriculum, including sex education.

Implementing sex education policies and programmes

Information for parents

35. In order to secure maximum support for their programmes of sex education, schools should ensure that both current and prospective parents are fully informed of the content of these programmes and of how they can play a part in influencing the development or review of these. Information about sex education must be included in the school's prospectus; and governors are required to make and keep up to date a statement of their policy on education, which must be made freely available to parents. Schools should also ensure that parents understand the right of withdrawal and how to exercise it (see below).

The right of withdrawal

36. Section 241 of the Education Act 1993 gives parents the right to withdraw their children from any or all parts of a school's programme of sex education, **other than those elements which are required by the National Curriculum Science Order** (see paragraphs 16, 17, 20 and 23-25 above). This parental right of withdrawal extends to all pupils attending maintained schools, including those over compulsory school age. A pupil in the latter category who sought to challenge the parental decision would, if he or she could not resolve the matter with the parents, ultimately have to apply to the courts. Parents do not have to give reasons for their decision; nor do they have to indicate what other arrangements they intend to make for providing sex education for the children. Once a request that a child be excused has been made, that request must be complied with until the parent changes or revokes it.

37. Schools should therefore ensure that the arrangements they

make for the submission of such requests are straightforward and easily understood. They should avoid putting any pressure on parents who decide to exercise this right. They may, however, invite parents voluntarily to indicate their reasons for withdrawal, so that any misunderstandings about the nature of the sex education provided by the school can be resolved. Where a parent wishes to discuss with the school possible ways of providing sex education at home, the Secretary of State hopes that schools will be ready to offer appropriate support, information and help, perhaps by recommending particular written materials on various aspects of sex education (including education about HIV, AIDS and other sexually transmitted diseases) that parents may find helpful.

Advice to individual pupils

38. It is important to distinguish between, on the one hand, the school's function of providing education generally about sexual matters on the basis described above, and, on the other, counselling and advice to individual pupils on these issues, particularly if this relates to their own sexual behaviour. Good teachers have always taken a pastoral interest in the welfare and well-being of pupils. But this function should never trespass on the proper exercise of parental rights and responsibilities.

39. Particular care must be exercised in relation to contraceptive advice to pupils under 16, for whom sexual intercourse is unlawful. The general rule must be that giving an individual pupil advice on such matters without parental knowledge or consent would be an inappropriate exercise of a teacher's professional responsibilities. Teachers are not health professionals, and the legal position of a teacher giving advice in such circumstances has never been tested in the courts.

40. Accordingly a teacher approached by an individual pupil for specific advice on contraception or other aspects of sexual behaviour should, wherever possible, encourage the pupil to seek advice from his or her parents, and, if appropriate, from the relevant health service professional (e.g., the pupil's GP or the school doctor or nurse). Where the circumstances are such as to lead the teacher to believe that the pupil has embarked upon, or is contemplating, a course of conduct which is likely to place him or her at moral or physical risk or in breach of the law, the teacher has a general responsibility to ensure that the pupil is aware of the implications and is urged to seek advice as above. In such circumstances, the teacher should inform the head teacher. The head teacher should

arrange for the pupil to be counselled if appropriate and, where the pupil is under age, for the parents to be made aware, preferably by the pupil himself or herself (and in that case checking that it has been done). Whether the specialist support services (including school health professionals) or the local education authority should also be involved will depend upon the particular circumstances involved and the professional judgement of the staff.

41. In deciding whether to deal with the provision of individual advice and counselling in their policy on sex education, governing bodies should bear these considerations in mind.

42. Guidance on the action to be taken in cases of suspected child abuse, and the role of schools in educating pupils about how to keep safe, was given in Circular 4/88 and in the booklet on inter-agency guidance, "Working Together under the Children Act" which was issued in October 1991.

Teacher in-service training

43. Schools will need to review the adequacy of the training which those teachers who have the major responsibility for providing sex education have undertaken ...

Annex C

Guidance on good practice in developing a school sex education policy

The following guidance suggests the processes by which a school governing body might develop or review its policy on sex education. It applies to both primary and secondary schools, although the steps would need to be modified in the case of a primary school which exercised its discretion not to provide sex education.

Eight successive steps are described:

1. Reviewing existing policy and practice
2. Identifying the pupils' needs
3. Identifying staff and wider community needs
4. Drafting the policy or policy changes
5. Consultation
6. Communication
7. Implementing the policy
8. Monitoring the implementation of the policy

Schools may wish to consider whether to assign the first three or four steps to a small group of governors and staff, and to involve a wider group in the remaining steps. Between steps 3 and 4 it will be necessary to reach decisions in principle on the aims and objectives of the policy and the main points of substance to be reflected in the policy statement.

Note:

The Circular specifies the steps to be taken in further detail and provides a 'Moral Framework for Written Policy Statement'. These are omitted from this book because of constraints on space.

Appendix 2

Schedule of cases

AG v *Guardian Newspapers Ltd (No.2)* [1988] 3 All ER 545
Attorney General's Reference No.1 of 1975 [1975] QB 773
Carey v *Population Services* 431 U.S. 678 (1977)
Carroll, Re [1931] 1 KB 317
C (A Minor) (Leave to Seek Residence Order) [1994] 1 FLR 26
Cumings v *Birkenhead Corporation* [1972] Ch.12
E (A Minor) (Wardship: Medical Treatment), Re [1993] 1 FLR 386
Fretwell (1862) Le & Ca 161
F v *Wirral MBC* [1991] 2 WLR 1132
Gillick v *West Norfolk and Wisbech Area Health Authority and Another* [1985] 3 All ER 402; [1986] AC 112
G (Parental Responsibility: Education), Re [1995] 2 FLR 53
Hedley Byrne & Co v *Heller and Partners* [1964] A.C. 465
Hoffman v *Austria* [1993] Publ. Eur. Ct. H.R. Series A, No.255C
Keegan v *Ireland* [1994] Publ. Eur. Ct. H.R. Series A, No.290
Kjeldsen, Busk Madsen and Pederson v *Denmark* [1976] 1 EHRR 711; 7 December Series A No.23
Krishnan v *Sutton L.B.C.* [1970] Ch.181
Jane v Jane (1983) FLR 712
M (A Minor) (Child: Wishes and Feelings), Re [1995] 2 FLR 90
M v *M (Minor) (Jurisdiction), Re* (1992) Fam Law 396
NCB v *Gamble* [1959] 1 QB 11
Neville Estates Ltd v *Madden* [1961] 3 All ER 769
O (A Minor) (Medical Treatment), Re [1993] 2 FLR 149
P (A Minor) (Education), Re [1992] 1 FLR 316
R (A Minor) (Wardship: Consent to Treatment), Re [1992] Fam. 11
R v *Bainbridge* [1960] 1 QB 129
R (Child Abduction: Acquiescence), Re [1993] 1 FLR 716
R v *Moloney* [1985] AC 905
R v *Tyrell* [1894] 1 QB 710
S (A Minor) (Medical Treatment), Re [1993] 2 FLR 376

S, Re [1992] 2 FLR 313
SC (A Minor) (Leave to Seek Residence) [1994] 1 FLR 96
Smith v *Ricci 459 U.S. 962* (1992)
W (A Minor) (Medical Treatment: Court's Jurisdiction), Re [1992] 3 WLR 758
Ware v *Valley Stream H.S. Dist* (1989) 545 N.Y.S. 2d at 320
Watt v *Kesteven C.C.* [1955] 1 A11 ER 473

Bibliography

Adame, D (1985) 'On the effects of sex education'. *Health Education*, 6, 8-10

Akhtar, S (1989) *Be careful with Muhammad!* Bellew Publishing

Allen, I (1987) *Education in Sex and Personal Relationships*. Policy Studies Institute

Allen, I (1991) *Family Planning and Pregnancy Counselling projects for young people*. Policy Studies Institute

Alston, P, Parker S and Seymour J (1992) *Children, Rights and the Law*. Oxford University Press

Ashworth, A (1991) *Principles of Criminal Law*. Clarendon Press

Auld Committee (1984) *The Shops Act: Late-Night and Sunday Opening: Report of the Committee of Inquiry into Proposals to Amend the Shops Act*. Cmnd 9376. HMSO

Bainham, A (1988) *Children, Parents and the State*. Sweet & Maxwell

Bainham, A (1993) *Children: The Modern Law*. Jordan

Bainham, A (1994) '"See you in Court Mum": Children as Litigants', 6 *Journal of Child Law*, 127

Bainham, A (1995) 'Family Law in a Pluralistic Society'. *Journal of Law and Society*, 22, 2, 234

Balding, J and Regis, D (1991) 'What do young people know about AIDS?' *Education and Health*, 9, 1, 12-15

Baldo, M, Aggleton, P and Slutkin, G (1993) *Does Sex Education lead to Earlier or Increased Sexual Activity in Youth*? Paper presented at the June 1993 WHO Berlin Conference on AIDS as part of the World Health Organisation Global Programme on AIDS

Bash, L and Coulby, D *eds* (1989) *The Education Reform Act: Competition and Control*. Cassell

Bell, J (1990) 'Religious Observance in Secular Schools: The French Solution' 2 (3) *Education and the Law*, 121

Beloff QC, M and Mountfield, H (1994) *Joint Opinion: Sex Education in Schools*. Association of Teachers and Lecturers.

Bhopal, R and Donaldson, L (1988) 'Health Education for Ethnic Minorities'. *Health Education Journal*, 47, 137

Blakey, V and Pullen, E (1991) 'You Don't Have to Say You Love Me: An Evaluation of a Drama-Based Sex Education Project for Schools'. *Health Education Journal*, 50, 161

Bradney, A (1985) 'Judging Families'. *Family Law*, 15, 168

Bradney, A (1987) 'Separate Schools, Ethnic Minorities and the Law'. *New Community*, 13, 412

Bradney, A (1993) *Religion, Rights and Laws*. Leicester University Press

Brazier, M (1992) *Medicine, Patients and the Law* Penguin Books

Britton, P (1993) 'Education through Ignorance'. *Index on Censorship*, 1, 11-12

Burghes, L (1994) 'Teenage sex and sex education' *Family Policy Studies Bulletin*. May

Carabine, J (1992) '"Constructing women": women's sexuality and social polity'. *Critical Social Policy*, 34, Summer, 23-37

Central Statistical Office (1995) *Social Trends*. Central Statistical Office

Commission of the European Communities (1991) *AIDS Research within the Biomedical and Health Research Programme*. Medical Research Division, SDME 2.46, Brussels

Coulby, D (1990) 'The National Curriculum' in Bash, L and Coulby, D *The Education Reform Act: Competition and Control*, Cassell

Craft, A (1987) *Mental Handicap and Sexuality: Issues and Perspectives*, Costello

Craft, A (*ed.*) (1993) *Practice Issues in Sexuality and Learning Disabilities,* International Thomson

Darlington, S (1994) 'Ignorance is not bliss'. *Education*, 29 April, 329

Davidson, N (1990) *Boys Will Be...? Sex Education and Young Men*. Bedford Square Press

Dennis, I H, 'The Mental Element for Accessories' in Smith, P *ed.* (1987) *Essays in Honour of J C Smith*. Butterworths

DES (1985) *Better Schools*. Cmnd 9469. DES

DES (1987) Circular 11/87, *Sex Education at School*. DES

DFE (1993a) (April), *Sex Education in Schools* (Draft Circular). DFE

DFE (1993b) Draft Circular, *Sex Education in Schools*. DFE

DFE (1994) *Education Act 1993: Sex Education in Schools* (Circular 5/94). DFE

DFE/Welsh Office (1994) *Code of Practice – on the identification and assessment of special educational needs*. DFE/Welsh Office

DFEE (1995) (July), Press Release 147/95. DFEE

DoE (1988) *Local Government Act 1988* (Circular 12/88). DoE

DoE (1994) *Access to Local Authority and Housing Association Tenancies*. DoE

Douglas, G (1991) *Law, Fertility and Reproduction*. Sweet and Maxwell

Doyal, L 'HIV AND AIDS: Putting Women on the Global Agenda' in Doyal, L, Naidoo, J and Wilton, T *eds* (1994) *AIDS: Setting a Feminist Agenda*. Taylor and Francis

Dummett, A (1986) 'Race, Culture and Moral Education'. *Journal of Moral Education*, 15, 10

Dworkin, R (1984) 'Rights as Trumps' in Waldron, J *Theories of Rights*. Oxford University Press

Eekelaar, J (1986a) 'The Emergence of Children's Rights'. *Oxford Journal of Legal Studies*, 6, 161

Eekelaar, J (1986b) 'The Eclipse of Parental Rights'. *Law Quarterly Review*, 102, 4

Farrell, C and Kellaher, L (1978) *My Mother Said... The way young people learned about sex and birth control*. Routledge & Kegan Paul

Feldman, D (1993) *Civil Liberties and Human Rights in England and Wales*. Clarendon Press

Francombe, C and Walsh, J (1995) *Young Teenage Pregnancy*. Middlesex University

Freeman, M D A (1983) *The Rights and Wrongs of Children*. Frances Pinter

Garden, N (1988) *Annie on my Mind*. Virago Upstarts

Garnham, A and Knights, K (1993) *Putting the Treasury First: The Truth about Child Support*. Child Poverty Action Group

Goldman, R and Goldman, J (1982) *Children's Sexual Thinking*. Routledge and Kegan Paul

Gordon, S, Scales, P and Everyley, K *eds* (1972) *The Sexual Adolescent: communication with teenagers about sex* (second edition). US, North Scituate, Mass.: Duxbury Press

Graham, D with Tytler, D (1993) *A Lesson for Us All – The Making of the National Curriculum*. Routledge

Gregory, J (1987) *Sex, Race and the Law*. Sage

Harris, N (1990) 'Education by Right? Breach of the Duty to Provide "Sufficient" Schools'. *Modern Law Review* 53, 4, 525-5

Harris, N (1992) *Complaints About Schooling*. National Consumer Council

Harris, N (1993) *Law and Education: Regulation, Consumerism and the Education System*. Sweet and Maxwell

Harris, N (1995) *The Law Relating to Schools* (2nd ed). Tolley

Harris, N, Pearce, P and Johnstone, S (1992) *The Legal Context of Teaching*. Longman

Helweg, A (1979) *Sikhs in England*. Oxford University Press

Holland, J, Ramazanoglu, C and Scott, S (1990) 'Managing risk and experiencing danger: tensions between government AIDS education policy and young women's sexuality'. *Gender and Education*, 2, 2, 125-146

Holland, J, Ramazanoglu, C and Sharpe, S (1993) *Wimp or Gladiator: Contradictions in acquiring masculine sexuality*. Tufnell Press

Holly, L 'My Nan said, "Sure you're not pregnant": Schoolgirl Mothers' in Holly, L *ed*. (1989) *Girls and Sexuality*. Oxford University Press

Holly, L 'Teaching sex: the experiences of four teachers' in Holly, L *ed*. (1989) *Girls and Sexuality*. OUP

Honigsbaum, N (1991) *HIV, AIDS and Children: A Cause for Concern*. National Children's Bureau

Houghton-James, H (1994) 'Children Divorcing Parents'. *Journal of Social Welfare and Family Law*, 185

House of Commons Health Select Committee (1993) Fourth Report 1990-91, *Maternity Services: Preconception*. HC 430. HMSO

IQRA (1991) *Meeting the Needs of Muslim Pupils*. IQRA Trust

Jeffrey, P (1979) *Frogs in a Well*. Zed Press

Johnson, A M and others (1994) *Sexual Attitudes and Lifestyles*, Blackwell Scientific

Jones, E F and others (1985) 'Teenage pregnancy in developed countries: determinants and policy implications'. *Family Planning Perspectives*, 17, 2, 53-63

Jones, E F and others (1986) *Teenage Pregnancy in Industrialised Countries: A Study Sponsored by the Alan Guttmacher Institute*. Yale University Press

Jones, M (1992) 'Teenage pregnancies: who is responsible?', *Education and Health*, 10, 2, 21-24

Kirby, D (1995) 'Sex and HIV/AIDS Education in Schools'. British Medical Journal, 311, 403

Kirby, D and others (1994) 'School based programmes to reduce sexual risk behaviours: a review of effectiveness'. *Public Health Reports*, 109, 3, 339-360

Knott, K (1986) *Religion and Identity, and the Study of Ethnic Minority Religions in Britain*. University of Leeds Community Religions Project

Knott, K and Khokher, K (1993) 'Young Muslim Women in Bradford'. *New Community*, 19, 593

Lees, S (1994) 'Talking about sex in sex education'. *Gender and Education*, 6, 3. 281-292

Lenskyj, H (1990) 'Beyond plumbing and prevention: feminist approaches to sex education'. *Gender and Education*, 3, 3, 291-309

Levy QC, A (1994) *Opinion: Re DFE Draft Guidelines on Sex Education*. National Children's Bureau

Lind, C and Butler, C (1995) 'The Legal Abuse of Homosexual Children?' *Journal of Child Law*, 7, 1, 3-9

Lowe, N and Juss, S (1993) 'Medical Treatment – Pragmatism and the Search for Principle'. *Modern Law Review* 56, 865

Lowe, N V and White, R A H (1979) *Wards of Court*, Butterworth

Mac An Ghaill, M (1991) 'Schooling, sexuality and male power: towards an emancipatory curriculum'. *Gender and Education*, 3, 3, 291-309

Macnair, M.R.T. (1989) 'Homosexuality in schools – Section 28, Local Government Act 1988'. *Education and the Law* 1, 1, 35

McCall Smith, A (1990) 'Is Anything Left of Parental Rights?' in Sutherland, E and McCall Smith, A eds *Family Law and Medical Advance*. Edinburgh University Press

McDermott, M and Ahsan, M (1986) *The Muslim Guide*. The Islamic Foundation

Massey, D (1990) 'School Sex Education'. *Health Education Journal*, 49, 134

Mawdudi, A (1980) *Human Rights in Islam*. The Islamic Foundation

Meredith, P (1989) *Sex Education: Political Issues in Britain and Europe*. Routledge

Meredith, P (1992) *Government, Schools and the Law*. Routledge

Mill, (1972) *On Liberty*. J M Dent and Sons

Miller, A (1994) *Young people: sex education and sexual activity* (Report for BBC North-West) Liverpool John Moores University

Mills, J (1992) 'Classroom conundrums: sex education and censorship' in Segal, L and McIntosh, M eds *Sex Exposed: Sexuality and the Pornography Debate*. Virago

Modood, T (1988) 'Black', Racial Equality and Asian Identity, 14, 397

Morgan, J (1993) *What Parents Think Their Children Know – What Their Children Say They Know*. Quaestor

Mori (1991) *Young Adults: health and lifestyle reports*. HEA

Muslim Parliament (1992) *White Paper on Muslim Education in Great Britain*. The Muslim Parliament of Great Britain

National Curriculum Council (1990a) *Curriculum Guidance 5: Health Education*. National Curriculum Council

National Curriculum Council (1990b) *Curriculum Guidance 8: Education for Citizenship*. National Curriculum Council

National Curriculum Council (1993) *Spiritual and Moral Development – A Discussion* Paper National Curriculum Council

NFER (National Foundation for Educational Research) (HEA) (1993) *A Survey of Health Education Policies in Schools*. HEA

NFER (National Federation of Educational Research) (1994) *Parents, Schools and Sex Education*. HEA

Noibi, D (1993) *Islam* in Thomson, R ed. *Religion, Ethnicity and Sex Education*. National Children's Bureau

Oakley, A and others (1995) 'Sexual health education interventions for young people: a methodological review'. *British Medical Journal* 310, 158

O'Donovan, K (1985) *Sexual Divisions in Law*. Weidenfeld and Nicolson

OFSTED (1995) *The OFSTED Handbook: Guidance on the Inspection of Secondary Schools*. HMSO

OPCS (1991) *Monitor*. PP291/1. HMSO

OPCS (1992), *Birth Statistics Series*. FMI. HMSO

OPCS (1994a) *Birth Statistics Series*. FMI. HMSO

OPCS (1994b) *Population Trends*. 77 Autumn. HMSO

Panos Dossier 4 (1990) *Triple Jeopardy: Women and AIDS*. The Panos Institute

Parekh, B (1990) 'Britain and the Logic of Social Pluralism' in Commission for Racial Equality *Britain: a Plural Society*. Commission for Racial Equality

Petchesky, R P (1986) *Abortion and Woman's Choice*. Verso

Phelps, F, Melanby, A and Tripp, J (1992) 'So you really think you understand sex?' *Education and Health*, 10, 2, 27-31

PHLS AIDS Centre and CDEH (1994) AIDS/HIV *Quarterly Surveillance Tables*, No.22: Data to the end of December 1993

Piper, C (1994) 'Parental Responsibility and the Education Acts'. *Family Law* 24, 146

Plaskow (1988) 'A long view from the inside', in Plaskow *ed. Life and Death of the Schools Council*. Falmer

Rawls, J (1988) 'The Priority of the Rights and Ideas of the Good'. *Philosophy and Public Affairs*, 17, 251

Ray, C (1994) 'Sex Education' *Highlight*. National Children's Bureau

Ray, C and Went, D *eds* (1995) *Good Practice in Sex Education: A Sourcebook for Schools*. National Children's Bureau

Robinson, J (1992) 'Back to school and a White Paper'. *New Law Journal* 142 1190

Rodham, H (1973) 'Children under the Law'. *Harvard Educational Review*, 43, 487

Rudyat, K, Ryan, H and Speed, M (1992) *Today's Young Adults – 16 – 19-year-olds look at diet, alcohol, smoking, drugs and sexual behaviour*. Health Education Authority

Sadurski, W (1990) *Moral Pluralism and Legal Neutrality*. Kluwer

Sardar, Z and Wyn Davies (1990) *Distorted Imaginations*. Grey Seal Books

Sarwar, G (1989) *Sex Education: The Muslim Perspective*. Muslim Education Trust

Sarwar, G (1994) *British Muslims and Schools*. Muslim Educational Trust

Science Group *eds* (1980) *Alice Through the Microscope*. Virago

Scottish Law Commission, (1992) *No. 135 Report on Family Law*. HMSO

Secretary of State for Education/Welsh Secretary (1992) *Choice and Diversity: a new framework for schools*. Cm2021. HMSO

Secretary of State for Health (1991) *The Health of the Nation*. Cm1523. HMSO

Secretary of State for Health (1992) *The Health of the Nation – A strategy for health in England*. Cm1986. HMSO

Sex Education Forum (1992) *A Framework for School Sex Education*. National Children's Bureau

Sex Education Forum (1994) *Response to Circular 5/94: Sex Education in Schools*

Sex Education Forum (1995) *Response to Robert Whelan pamphlet Teaching sex in schools – does it work?*

Smith, J C and Hogan, B (1992) *Criminal Law*. Butterworths

Stafford, J M (1988) 'In defence of gay lessons'. *Journal of Moral Education*, 17, 1, January

Stonewall (1994) *Arrested Development*. Stonewall

Thomas, P A (1993) 'The nuclear family, ideology and AIDS in the Thatcher years'. *Feminist Legal Studies*, 1, 1, 23-44

Thomas, P and Costigan, R (1990) *Promoting Homosexuality: Section 28 of the Local Government Act 1988*. Cardiff Law School

Thomson, R *ed.* (1993) *Religion, Ethnicity and Sex Education: Exploring the Issues*. National Children's Bureau

Thomson, R (1994) 'Moral Rhetoric and Public Health Pragmatism: the Recent Politics of Sex Education'. *Feminist Review*, 48, Autumn 40-60

Thomson, R and Scott, S (1991) *Learning about sex: Young women and the social construction of sexual identity*. Tufnell Press

Thomson, R and Scott, L (1992) *An Enquiry into Sex Education*. National Children's Bureau

UN Committee on Rights of the Child (1995) *Report on the United Kingdom*, 208 stg, 26 January 1995, U.N.Doc.CRC/C/15/Add.34. UN

Walsh, V (1980) 'Contraception: The Growth of a Technology' in The Brighton Women & Science Group *eds Alice Through the Microscope*. Virago

Wellings, K and others (1994) *Sexual Behaviour in Britain. The National Survey of Sexual Attitudes and Lifestyles*. Penguin

Wellings, K and others (1995) 'Provision of sex education and early sexual experience: the relation examined'. *British Medical Journal*, 311, 417

Whelan, R (1995) *Teaching sex in schools – does it work?* Family Education Trust

Weyman, A (1993) 'The Fourth "R"', *Concern* 3, Autumn

White, S (1995) *Confidentiality in Schools Manual*. Brook Advisory Centres

Whitson, J A (1992) 'Sexuality and Censorship in the Cirriculum: Beyond Formalistic Legal Analysis' in Sears, J T *ed.*, *Sexuality and the Curriculum: The Politics and Practices of Sexuality Education*. New York: Teachers College Press

Whitty, G and Menter, I (1989) 'Lessons of Thatcherism: Education Policy in England and Wales 1979-88' (1989) *Journal of Law and Society* 16, 42

WHO (1994) *AIDS: images of the epidemic*. WHO

WHO (1995) 'The Correct Global situation of the HIV/AIDS Pandemic'. *Global programme on AIDS*, 3 July 1995. WHO site on the World Wide Web.

Wight, D (1993) 'A re-assessment of health education on HIV/AIDS for young heterosexuals'. *Health Education Research*, 8, 4, 473-483

Williams, H (1993) *Advice re: Sex Education in Schools: Proposed Revision of Circular 11/87*. Liberty

Wollstonecraft, M (1992) *A Vindication of the Rights of Women*. Penguin

Wolpe, A (1987) 'Sex in school: back to the future', *Feminist Review*, 27, 37-47

Yudof, M.D. and others (1982) *Educational Policy and the Law*. New York: McCutchan

Index

Entries are arranged in letter-by-letter order (hyphens and spaces between words are ignored). UK legislation has not been included in this index.

Publications

Recent works include:

Balancing the Act

Social Work and Assessment with Adolescents

Good Practice in Sex Education: A sourcebook for schools

Children's Rights and HIV

Managing to Change

Schools' SEN Policies Pack

Crossing the Boundaries

Growing Up

It's Your Meeting!

Intervention in the Early Years

The Bureau also publishes a quarterly journal, *Children & Society* – to subscribe please contact John Wiley & Sons,
Tel: 01243 770634 Fax: 01243 770638

For further information or a catalogue please contact:
Book Sales, National Children's Bureau, 8 Wakley Street,
London EC1V 7QE
Tel: 0171 843 6029 Fax: 0171 278 9512